10 SECRETS
I LEARNED FROM
THE APPRENTICE

10 SECRETS
I LEARNED FROM
THE APPRENTICE

UNAUTHORIZED EXPERT TIPS

Anthony Parinello with Beth Gottfried

An "Express Paperback"
Chamberlain Bros.
a member of Penguin Group (USA) Inc.
New York

Chamberlain Bros.
a member of
Penguin Group (USA) Inc.
375 Hudson Street
New York, NY 10014

An application has been submitted to register this book with the Library of Congress.

ISBN 1-59609-004-9

Printed in the United States of America

1 3 5 7 9 10 8 6 4 2

Book designed by Mike Rivilis.

CONTENTS

Introduction 1

Secret #1: Think Big. 7

Secret #2: Show the Competition No Mercy 15

Secret #3: Defend Yourself Aggressively 25

Secret #4: Remember, Consensus Is Overrated 33

Secret #5: Identify All Possible Resources,
and Use Them Strategically 41

Secret #6: Cut Your Losses 49

Secret #7: Get Face-to-Face
with Key Decision-Makers 57

Secret #8: Step Up—Take Intelligent Chances,
and Then Take Responsibility 65

Secret #9: Advance the Most Profitable Deal 73

Secret #10: Negotiate Tough;
Negotiate Based on Your Negotiating Partner's
Situation and Personality; Understand that
No Single Negotiating Strategy Is Perfect 81

The Ten Secrets Blueprint 88

Bonus Secret #1: Dressing for Success 93
Bonus Secret #2: Successful Executive Ettiquette 99
Bonus Secret #3: Speaking Successfully 104

Apprentice Musings by Beth Gottfried
    The Aftermath of *The Apprentice* 109
    The Battle of the Sexes in *The Apprentice* 112
    The Apprentice: A Personality Profile 116

The $100,000 Resource Guide 118

Recommended Reading 146

INTRODUCTION

Why bother learning the rules for success in the world of Donald Trump?

Because, like it or not, he matters.

In recent years, there has been a profusion of "top one hundred" lists prepared for the benefit of the viewing, reading, and Internet-surfing public. You've probably seen your fair share of them: The top one hundred entertainers of the decade, the top one hundred rock-and-roll guitarists of all time, the top one hundred situation comedy episodes ever filmed, and so on. When the history of the current decade is written, there will, inevitably, be a "top one hundred" list of Americans who had the greatest impact on popular culture—and another list showcasing those Americans who left their mark in the world of business. It is certain that both lists will include the name of Donald Trump.

Whether anyone could have predicted it or not, whether anyone likes it or not, Trump's image, his values, his strategies, and his personal style have had a profound and indelible effect on business and popular culture. He has become the icon of modern American success, or at least of success in material terms. He presents a distinctive mixture of win-at-all-costs chutzpah, creative thinking, and unapologetic self-promotion (self-promotion that is, we must acknowledge, aggressive even by American standards).

In case you need any convincing on that final point, consider the names the man has bestowed on his companies:

> Trump Hotels & Casino Resorts, Inc.; Trump Hotels & Casino Resorts Funding, Inc.; Trump Hotels & Casino Resorts Holdings, L.P.; Trump Atlantic City Holding, Inc.; Trump Atlantic City Associates; Trump Atlantic City Funding, Inc.; Trump Atlantic City Funding II, Inc.; Trump Atlantic City Funding III, Inc.; Trump Atlantic City Corporation; Trump Hotels & Casino Resorts Enterprises; Trump's Castle Funding, Inc.; Trump Marina, Inc.; Trump Hotels & Casino Resorts/LP Corporation; Trump Taj Mahal Associates; Trump Casinos, Inc.; Trump Casino Holdings, LLC; Trump Casino Funding, Inc.

Or pull up any catalogue of his real estate holdings:

> Trump World Tower; Trump Place; Trump Tower; Trump International Hotel and Tower; Trump Palace;

Trump Parc; Trump Plaza Hotel and Casino on the Boardwalk; Trump's Castle Casino Resort; Trump Taj Mahal.

And so on. Notice a pattern?

This relentlessly self-advancing (some might say self-obsessed) philosophy of business—a philosophy that demands the attention of the media—recalls the life of Charles Foster Kane, the hero of Orson Welles's classic film Citizen Kane. But there's a major difference: Trump is not a tragic figure. And as he cruises toward his sixtieth birthday, he shows, unlike Welles's crumbling media magnate, no signs whatsoever of having passed his peak. To the contrary, he seems to be hitting his stride before our very eyes.

Forbes magazine recently estimated Trump's personal wealth at a staggering $1.74 billion—not bad for someone who was, according to his detractors, on the brink of bankruptcy in the early 1990s. Perhaps predictably, Trump has insisted that this figure reflects not even half of his actual holdings.

Trump's initiative, skills, charm, and obstacle-obliterating confidence have allowed him not only to engineer one of the greatest business turnarounds in American history, but also to re-establish himself as a major, and widely respected, American brand. These days, being a major American brand means, as a general but reliable rule, that you are also a major *global* brand. So it is safe to say that people around the world are trying to emulate Donald Trump: not only his flamboyant lifestyle and promotional flair, but also, and perhaps more importantly, his strategies for running a business and managing a career.

What follows, then, are ten secrets for success in the workplace. Each is drawn from *The Apprentice*, the smash hit reality television program that already seems like an American institution. Like the Trump comeback itself, nobody managed to see the show's triumph coming ahead of time. Its addictive blend of brutal competition, manipulative head games, and ruthless bottom-line accountability has delivered huge ratings, in part because of the personality of the man at its center, but also because it imparts identifiable principles for setting and achieving important business goals.

Some may argue that a few of the strategies border on the Machiavellian, but these days that is what makes for entertaining television and, not infrequently, success in the boardroom.

It is theoretically possible that someone could garner high television ratings by creating a network reality show about a business based on the leadership secrets of a person like Pope John Paul II or Florence Nightingale. But let's face it: It's not very likely. The hard truth of the matter is that we are not always curious about the world's altruists—at least, we aren't interested in them when we want to launch a competition-crushing business, or eliminate a rival for a plum assignment, or watch others do these things. Instead, we look to people like Donald Trump. And if we take a close enough look at his world, we may come away with an unexpected feeling of respect. Whether we choose to admit it to ourselves or not, we wonder about people like Trump. We are curious about the practical lessons they can pass along to us, not merely because of the prospect of financial success, but also because of their extraordinary talents.

Trump may well be an egotist, as his detractors claim. But if he is, he is one of those egotists who consistently manages to make good, in spectacular fashion, on his claims. If you've ever wondered how he does it, read on.

SECRET

#1

Think Big

Only with absolute fearlessness can we slay the dragons of mediocrity that invade our gardens.

—George Lois,
legendary graphic designer

It may be possible to succeed in the business world by focusing obsessively on small, incremental ideas, or by methodically refining a series of low-level initiatives. It's fair to say, though, that you're unlikely to impress Donald Trump (or any number of similar people) by working this way.

Time is tight in today's business environment, and people who rise to the top tend to use the time at their disposal to seize attention by presenting and pursuing bold initiatives. If your goal is to gain the immediate favorable attention of a superior—or, for that matter, a consumer—you should not expect to succeed by embracing the conventional and building your ideas around the familiar. In the world of Trump, business success on a large scale is the only success worth pursuing, and this level of accomplishment is only possible for those who are willing to make a way of life out of challenging established preconceptions and proposing new and exciting methods. Presumably, this is how George and Carolyn, Trump's executive employees and the other major decision-makers on *The Apprentice*, rose to their powerful positions within Trump's companies. And it's certainly how Trump became one of the wealthiest and most recognizable moguls of our day.

The majority of today's notably successful entrepreneurs are those who have been willing to challenge the status quo. These men and women have pursued intriguingly oversized dreams and have offered startling new ideas to the world at large. If you want to build your career, or your company, on the Donald Trump model, it cannot hurt to imitate those in the business world who share his penchant for thinking big.

Trump audaciously—and with obvious joy—built a real estate empire around himself, forsaking the advice of the experts by creating a luxury brand around his own name. Focus groups probably warned him it was a dangerous idea, and focus groups can certainly serve their purpose, but at a certain point you have to look beyond their often-narrow view in order to implement the truly big ideas. Name it all after yourself—and live a life big enough for the headlines to promote the brand you've built. That's thinking big.

Thinking big overcomes complacency. It shakes up markets and organizations. It requires hard work. And it instantly identifies those people in the organization who are committed to delivering a truly stellar performance.

Big thinking, when engaged in as a way of life, has a way of overcoming doubters and criticism, both well intentioned and otherwise. Jeff Bezos's Amazon.com ignored the naysayers for years and ended up as a retail powerhouse that completely demolished existing models for running a store, online or offline. Once upon a time, you'll recall, Amazon's goal was to be the world's biggest bookstore. People scoffed, claimed the stock was overpriced, and called Bezos misguided for focusing obsessively on expansion. They said he couldn't turn a profit. Nowadays, that kind of talk has stopped, and Amazon.com's pull-down menu includes car parts, apparel, jewelry, gourmet food, cell phones, pet food—you name it.

While we're on the subject of thinking big, let's not forget the example of Sam Walton. Not too many years ago, business-school professors would have laughed at the idea of building a compelling brick-and-mortar retail concept around the idea of selling just about everything, at the lowest possible price. Wal-Mart proved them all wrong, and in doing so revolutionized the American retail scene.

It was business-school professors, we should remember, who counseled the founder of Federal Express that it wasn't prudent to try to create a business around the guaranteed overnight shipment of packages.

Trump's style is to launch, define, and operate his business—and his career—in a way that continually shatters people's preconceptions. This is an excellent style to emulate. It may mean introducing an entirely new product in a category that the experts have concluded simply does not exist; it may mean executing on a scale that has never even been considered; it may mean reaching out to consumers with a service that nobody else has bothered to offer. Whatever form it takes, this kind of thinking generally ignores the instinctive caution of naysayers.

Robert Kennedy once said, "About half of the people you run into will say no to anything that you suggest." He was talking about people in government, but the same principle applies in the corporate world. About half the people you run into avoid thinking big. It looks risky because it is risky. But it's not as risky—at least in Trump's world—as trying to survive by fading in to the wallpaper.

Most people in business do not achieve success on a large scale, because they avoid thinking big. They try to conform, to stick with the existing pattern, to avoid challenging the established way of doing things. The Trump model is to think on a grand scale, to be willing to rattle a few cages, and to take extreme action.

Which reputation would you rather have: the reputation of the person who plays it safe, or the reputation of the person who questions the rules?

Consider the advertising competition in *The Apprentice*, in which both teams had to develop an ad campaign for the Marquis Jet Card, a card that allows people to buy a certain number of hours of private jet service. Donny Deutsch, of the advertising agency Deutsch Inc., judged the task, and he chose Team Protégé's sexy, shocking ads because he thought they illustrated a big idea, an entirely new concept that the Marquis company might want to embrace. Team Versacorp, on the other hand, stuck with the status quo and created a conservative, traditional ad campaign. Their unwillingness to try something creative, different, and new lost them the challenge.

Corporate leaders are always on the lookout for people who can generate and act on new, energizing, and oversized ideas. If you make a habit of thinking big—not for ten minutes a day, but for every waking hour—you will eventually notice something interesting happening: People have a way of making room at the table for big thinkers.

Only by thinking on a scale that no one ever thought possible can you achieve in a way no one ever thought possible.

Learning to focus on extra-large goals isn't just a temporary expedient. It's the way some people train themselves to live their lives, the way to get past obstacles that make small-thinking colleagues shudder. Jean la Fontaine wrote, "Man is so made that when anything fires his soul, impossibilities vanish." Sound like anyone you've seen at the head of the conference table in the boardroom?

Secret #1:
Think Big

- Present and pursue bold initiatives.
- Pursue business success on a large scale—it's the only success worth pursuing.
- Be willing to challenge the status quo.
- Overcome complacency.
- Launch, define, and operate your business—and your career—in a way that continually shatters people's preconceptions.
- Remember: People have a way of making room at the table for big thinkers.
- Realize that small ideas rarely lead to large accomplishments.
- Don't forget that time is tight in today's business environment.
- Learn to imitate Trump and other notably successful entrepreneurs.

Fashion Faux Pas?

Were the women's outfits on the show appropriate for today's business environment? Many people don't think so. Consider these examples and situations:

- During the lemonade challenge, Tammy complained about her sore feet. If when the contestants dressed in the morning they had no idea what the day's task might be, was it really wise of her to wear mules with four-inch heels?

- At Deutsch Advertising, Ereka was wearing a pink, purple, and black scarf tied around her head. Is it proper to look similar to a fortune-teller at the office?

- After the Elizabeth Glaser Pediatric AIDS Foundation benefit auction, Omarosa claimed that Heidi had no class. Is it ironic that, while Heidi was defending herself against Omarosa's statement in an interview, what appeared to be a black bra was sticking out of the plunging neckline of her light blue sweater?

- When Katrina and Amy were waiting to enter the boardroom after the Atlantic City gambling challenge, wasn't it obvious that they were having a difficult time finding positions on the yellow couch that would work with their super-short skirts?

- Was it acceptable for the women to wear tube tops throughout the show?

What would your boss say about such attire?

SECRET

#2

Show the Competition No Mercy

**Show me a good loser
and I'll show you an idiot.**

—Leo Durocher,
*former manager of the Brooklyn Dodgers (1939-1946),
the New York Giants (1948-1955), the Chicago Cubs (1966-1972),
and the Houston Astros (1972-1973)*

It's not enough to identify your company's competition and neutralize it. To play like Trump plays, you must also be willing to identify and neutralize your own competition as well.

This, of course, is the principle on which *The Apprentice* is based. Not only did the teams have to compete with one another for rewards and immunity, they also had to directly compete with the other members of their team. There could only be one winner, after all.

Not everyone considers it polite to mention, but we face two kinds of competition in the business world: *internal* and *external.* If you doubt this, consider the world of sports. To win a World Series ring, a baseball player must overcome both internal and external competition. The external competition is what the world sees, understands, recognizes, and celebrates: the seven-game contest between the two league champions. But how many people understand the internal competition that makes that high-level external competition possible?

Think of your own favorite team. Imagine the starting right fielder being named the Most Valuable Player of the World Series. He didn't get the opportunity to make that extraordinary contribution at that very high level by accident. To win a starting spot in his team's lineup, that right fielder had to defeat other players for the chance to start in right field and to show what he could do. And he had to do that on purpose. Even in a team sport, such as baseball, individual initiative is what makes team accomplishment possible. It's easy to forget that the person who starts in right field in the seventh game of the World Series has defeated not only all the rival outfielders on his team, but also all the rival outfielders in the team's minor-league system, as well as all the rival outfielders he encountered in the semipro ranks. And that's before we even take into account all the players that same right fielder had to overcome in college, high school, and Little League.

In business, as in sports, achievement is competitive on both the individual and the group level. If you ignore the competition, you ignore the achievement. To be sure, collaboration is important, but to win a team needs leaders, and people must compete energetically for leadership spots in a company, just as companies must compete energetically for leadership spots within a market. To pretend that collaboration can take the place of healthy, vigorous competition—whether it be for the job of starting right fielder or senior vice president of marketing—is simply naïve. In order to become the apprentice, Bill Rancic had to consciously compete against each of the other contestants, from David to Omarosa to Amy to Kwame, and everyone that came in between. If he'd been focused purely on helping his team, rather than on helping himself *and* his team, he wouldn't have ended up as the ultimate winner.

To succeed in Trump's world, you must show your company's competition no mercy. And you must show your own competition, on the individual level, no mercy. Lots of people are comfortable with the notion of harnessing every possible resource to take on their external competitors, to try to beat another team. But those same people often use words like "ruthless," "overaggressive," and "self-obsessed" to describe coworkers who strive to eliminate internal rivals. This is why some of the show's contestants were shocked when their teammates turned on them in the boardroom in an effort to stick up for themselves. But in the business world, the desire to finish on top is not self-obsessed—it is healthy. While it is always good to support your coworkers when the situation calls for it, you must remember that your ultimate concern is you.

If you are a person who wants to beat the other company

to market, win customers from the other company, and out-think the other company, then you must, by definition, also want the strongest possible team in place at your own company. How else can you expect to achieve your goals? The fateful question then arises: Do you want to be a leader on that team, or a follower?

We do not always like acknowledging, to ourselves or to other people, that we face competitors within our own organization. But we do. If you think it's possible to gain prominence and influence within your organization by sitting back and letting others take away the attention you deserve, the resources you need, or the credit for your work and ideas, then you are in for a disappointment.

And by the way, if you believe that people within your organization are not willing to take credit for your work, adopt your ideas, or sabotage your ambitions, then you probably have not been inside a boardroom lately. Kristi forgot this principle when, after her team failed the flea-market task and ended up actually losing money, she followed Jessie's advice about how to act in the boardroom. Jessie counseled her to keep quiet when Trump and her other teammates attacked her. But when Jessie turned on Kristi in the boardroom and Kristi kept quiet, she was fired. Kristi had forgotten that Jessie was looking out for herself. As she should have been.

In the world of the high achiever, competition is a rule of life. Just like on *The Apprentice*, the aim is to win, both on the personal and organizational levels: to win fairly and play by the rules, but to come in first, without apologizing for wanting to do so. In order to win, you have to be willing to out-work, out-think, out-promote, and, yes, outmaneuver people who desire the same things you do.

In the seventh episode, each of the two teams had to rent a Brooklyn apartment, renovate it, and then re-rent it at a higher price. Troy realized that he and Katrina, the project managers, would both want to rent the same apartment. Rather than flipping a coin for the right to make the first offer, as Troy suggested, Katrina insisted that they reveal their preferred choice on little pieces of paper, because she was worried that Troy would steal her idea. Instead of writing his chosen apartment, Troy wrote "I want what you want," thus perfectly outmaneuvering Katrina. He knew it couldn't affect the final outcome of the challenge, but he also knew it would make her lose her composure—which it did.

Success has a pattern: It always involves learning what must be done in order to outperform other people and other institutions. The instincts that motivate us to outperform other people are the same instincts that allow our organizations to outperform their corporate rivals. If you don't compete well at the individual level, you should not expect to be placed in charge of coordinating the competition at the group level. It's that simple.

When you are working within a team, of course you must pull together as a team and make all the contributions you possibly can. This was one of Omarosa's major problems: By neglecting to focus on her team, she made a very negative impression on the decision-makers as well as on much of the viewing audience. But by the same token, you must never forget that your goal is to become a leader, because you inevitably will be evaluated as an individual. Find the areas in which you will be able to make a contribution that is more tangible, more significant, and more compelling than the contribution of your rivals. Think twice before you hand a career rival an opportunity to shine in an area in which you know for a fact that you can make a leadership contribution.

Don't hold grudges. But don't hold anything back, either. In order to lead, you must focus with intensity on identifying the very best ways to win. If you don't, your competition will.

In business, as in sports,

achievement is competitive on both

the individual and the group level. If

you ignore the competition, you

ignore the achievement.

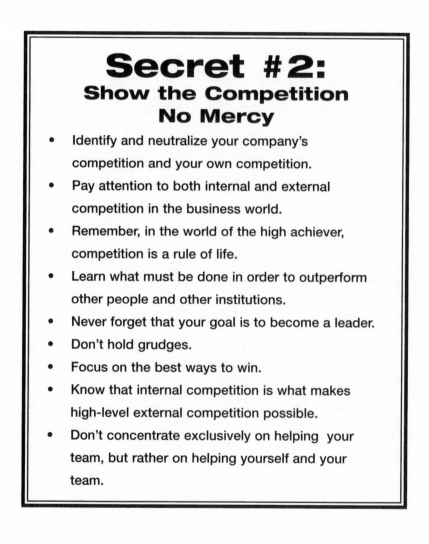

Secret #2:
Show the Competition No Mercy

- Identify and neutralize your company's competition and your own competition.
- Pay attention to both internal and external competition in the business world.
- Remember, in the world of the high achiever, competition is a rule of life.
- Learn what must be done in order to outperform other people and other institutions.
- Never forget that your goal is to become a leader.
- Don't hold grudges.
- Focus on the best ways to win.
- Know that internal competition is what makes high-level external competition possible.
- Don't concentrate exclusively on helping your team, but rather on helping yourself and your team.

AN APPRENTICE ASIDE:

The Truth About
the Brooklyn Apartment

In the seventh episode, when each team had to rent out a Brooklyn apartment, renovate it, and re-rent it for as much money as possible, it looked like Team Versacorp would win. But at the very last minute, a woman rented Team Protégé's apartment for a higher price, and they won the challenge.

However, the woman who rented the apartment has written that she was already planning to rent the apartment before it was on the show. She only accepted the deal with Team Protégé because the building's actual landlord had secretly promised that he'd drop the rent back down to the original price afterward.

SECRET

#3

Defend Yourself
Aggressively

Man never made any material
as resilient as the human spirit.
—Bernard Williams,
English philosopher

This is a partner idea to Secret #2, and should be used in harmony with it.

Life in the world of business is not always easy; most people know that. What seems to come as a surprise to many people who aspire to leadership positions, however, is the equally obvious fact that life in the world of business is not, and probably never will be, fair. The closest we can come to making it fair is to stand on our own two feet and defend ourselves and our ideas aggressively. If we wish to be seen as leaders, we cannot expect others to defend us. We have to do that job ourselves.

Can you think of the last political candidate who earned your respect by complaining about how unfair the world was, or by appealing to someone else for help? It's pretty difficult to imagine voters enthusiastically casting ballots for a whiner.

Now look at the other end of the continuum. Can you remember a political candidate who attracted your positive interest by responding with focused, controlled intensity to an attack from an opponent or a member of the news media? For most people, that kind of example is a little easier to recall. We expect children to talk about the unfairness of things, to run to others to settle their disputes. This is why some of the complaints made by a few of the contestants on *The Apprentice* seemed so immature. We expect leaders to respond to attacks, to set clear limits, and to defend themselves and their positions—on their own.

What we expect from politicians, senior executives expect from us.

When Omarosa belittled Jessie and Heidi in the boardroom after their team had made less money in the AIDS benefit auction, Trump was visibly shocked that they didn't defend themselves. He would have respected them more if they had, and this weakness was the major factor in the firing of Jessie. He expected her to stand up for herself.

It's only logical. If you were in serious legal trouble and had to pick a lawyer to keep you out of jail, would you prefer the attorney who was cautious, tentative, careful of every step, and retiring in demeanor? Or the one who tackled inaccuracies and false charges about you head-on, with power and conviction? If you're like most people, you would select the fighter. And guess what? Juries tend to respond most favorably to lawyers who defend their positions with enthusiasm, energy, and emotion. Juries assume that these lawyers know what they're talking about.

Corporate leaders, as a general rule, take the same approach when choosing the people who will represent their companies that you would take when picking an attorney to represent you. Corporate executives tend to assume that people who can defend themselves and their ideas have studied the competition, looked at all the options, and thought their plans through ahead of time. During the advertising task, when Donny Deutsch tried to dismiss Team Protégé's direct mail campaign for the jet card, Omarosa wouldn't let him. She enthusiastically defended and promoted their plan, and this strong defense contributed to Protégé's winning of the challenge.

Yes, there is an element of theater here. You have to address perceptions as well as realities. Scapegoating, rivalry, and sneak attacks can and will appear on the job, even if you do nothing to encourage them. The fact that you do not deserve these problems may or may not be obvious to the people in your organization whose actions will determine your professional destiny. These people may not notice, or have any interest in, the "injustice" of the situation as you perceive it. The only thing you can really expect them to notice is your own ability to respond effectively to whatever's just been dumped in your lap.

Right or wrong, the way you respond to an attack or a

challenge will be seen as an indicator of the way you will respond to the stressful situations that are part and parcel of a leadership role. There's a saying that has been expressed in hundreds of different ways in dozens of different cultures: A person's true character emerges under stress. Whether it's true or not (and it probably is), this adage guides people's judgments about you.

Which aspect of your personality emerges when you are placed in the stressful situation of having your ideas, your character, or your integrity attacked?

Forget about "rising above the fray." Forget about "ignoring charges that do not deserve a response." Forget about "letting the others do the fighting." If you are the one under attack, you, as an individual, have an obligation to yourself to step forward and state your case. Failing to do so may encourage more (and more outrageous) attacks—and may lead people in authority to assume that you lack the spirit to compete. That's not an impression you want to give.

In the boardroom, after Team Versacorp had lost the Planet Hollywood challenge by failing to make enough money at the restaurant that day, Kwame blamed Nick for the outcome. But Nick stepped up and defended himself. And he wasn't fired. In contrast, when Kristi was in the boardroom, after being project manager of the flea-market challenge, she didn't defend herself. And she was fired.

We live in a world where people will measure our confidence—and the value of our ideas—by our willingness and ability to defend ourselves. The fact that we know we are right counts for little or nothing. We must be willing to express *why* we are right, and to do so with passion.

The inability to provide a reasoned, well-articulated, and impassioned defense of what you believe in will inevitably be perceived as a sign of weakness—and perceptions count. It is a rare project plan indeed that is so strong that its merits will speak for themselves.

Make no mistake—in the world of Trump, you will be attacked. That is a given. Don't waste precious time complaining to someone that the attack was not fair and then expecting others to take up your defense. Don't waste precious time wishing you had anticipated the nature or direction of the attack. Don't waste precious time celebrating the defense you planned against another attack you thought you would face but did not. Deal with this attack. Leaders must come to grips with the fact that attacks come from all sides. Leaders know that they cannot possibly expect to anticipate the specifics of every attack. In the final challenge, when Bill was in charge of the Chrysler Trump Golf Tournament, he came under attack by some members of the golf course staff for his choice of storage location for the many gift items and signs he'd need for the tournament. Instead of making a big deal out of the attack, Bill just dealt with it, which is exactly how a leader should behave.

Failing to predict an attack is not a mistake. The mistake is expecting attacks to diminish or disappear by letting them go unanswered.

Secret #3:
Defend Yourself Aggressively

- Don't expect others to defend you.

- Remember, life in the business world is not always fair.

- Study the competition, look at all the options, and think your plans through ahead of time.

- Expect others to notice your ability to respond effectively to situations.

- If you're under attack, step forward and state your case.

- Hone the ability to provide a reasoned, well-articulated, and impassioned defense of what you believe in.

- Don't expect attacks to disappear by letting them go unanswered.

- Forget about "rising above the fray," "ignoring charges that do not deserve a response," and "letting others do the fighting."

AN APPRENTICE ASIDE:

Team Names

The Terrible Team Name Award goes to the women for thinking up "Protégé Corporation." And Versacorp—could the men have been any less original? One of Omarosa's suggestions, "Donald's Darlings," would have been even worse, proving that Amy was wrong: Some ideas actually are too stupid.

SECRET #4

Remember, Consensus is Overrated

*The best preparation for tomorrow is simply
to do today's work superbly well.*
—Sir William Osler,
English physician (1849-1919)

Have you ever had to work with a colleague whose goal in life seemed to be dicussing or evaluating any good idea to death?

Evaluating an idea to death is actually a pretty common occurrence in the business world. It usually results in a concept that has been watered down enough for all the members of a committee to be able to agree on it. The problem is that the initiative everyone can agree on very rarely equals the same initiative that can deliver optimum results. This situation is often referred to as "paralysis by analysis."

If the group can't agree on an outcome, it's better for the leader, or someone with leadership qualities, to make the final decision, rather than waiting for the group to come up with a mediocre compromise. This is how Nick handled things when he was project manager of the art task in the ninth episode of *The Apprentice*, in which each team had to set up an exhibition for a young artist and then try to make the most money from the sale of his or her artwork. Bill and Amy preferred Leah's caricature-style portraits, but Nick and Katrina liked Andrei's abstract forest art. Instead of waiting for the entire group to agree, Nick simply made an executive decision and chose Andrei. And Nick's team won.

Some people place way too much faith in the power of a committee. This is not Trump's approach to building a business or a career, and it shouldn't be yours, either.

If your aim is to take control of your own career, and to rise to the top of your organization, you should think twice before granting too much authority to any group, even a group of so-called "experts." When it comes to the critical decisions you and you alone are responsible for making, there can be no substitute for following the course you personally believe to be best.

Get the information you need from the experts and the key people who have the background and data you need. But don't let the meetings fool you into thinking that someone other than you is responsible for making the final call. If you're in charge of a project, don't rely on consensus. In the world of Trump, consensus is—or at least can be— a dirty word.

Though Trump took the advice of his colleagues into account when he evaluated each of the show's contestants, in the end he was the one firing and hiring people. The final choice had to be his, and his alone.

Your undertaking, your campaign, your career—these are, at the end of the day, your business and no one else's. Ultimately, the results of your initiative will be based on one person's decisions, outlooks, and analyses: yours. At the end of the day, you will be the one who will be asked about the reasons for the actions and methods you put forward. Not the experts. Not the committee. Not the team. The leader: you.

Anyone who loses sight of this principle is not likely to be a high achiever.

And this is why the project managers on *The Apprentice* received such a large portion of the praise, and the blame, that was doled out in the boardroom. At the end of the day, they were responsible for the final results of their team.

There's a very simple reason you should be dubious of granting groups too much authority. Groups tend to analyze rather than to act, and overanalysis is a recipe for disaster.

Analysis has its place, of course. There are certainly going to be critical technical questions and sudden, unexpected challenges that will benefit, for a time, from a group focus. It can be instructive—and essential—to collect the opinions of various team members who have specialized knowledge in areas that you don't. In the final analysis, however, you must always remember that the group you consult is not infallible.

Speaking generally, groups are less likely than individuals to develop initiatives that:

- transcend the problem of "paralysis by analysis"
- challenge existing preconceptions
- identify new market opportunities
- reflect a powerful, dynamic vision of the future
- anticipate problems that the organization has never before experienced
- require significant sacrifices by key constituencies within the organization

Perhaps the most dangerous consequence of management by consensus is known as group-think. When a team succumbs to group-think, it is likely to have an unjustified level of confidence in its own assessments of reality, and an unhealthy attachment to the imagined merits of the status quo. Group-think is the opposite of creativity, and it's not the way breakout companies operate.

It is a delusion to imagine that the wisdom of the group can protect us from the perils involved in taking personal responsibility for difficult decisions. Only one person will be held accountable for the deliberations of the group, and that person must be ready, willing, and able to ignore the consensus if he or she sees a reason to do so. Of course, the leader must also be willing to take responsibility if the decision results in a disaster—but that is the case whether you decide to convene the committee or not.

No amount of analysis or research can obscure the true role of an executive: to make decisions. Use the committee as a tool for securing insights and information you don't have so you can make an informed decision—don't use it as an excuse to avoid making decisions in the first place. If you're not comfortable with this amount of responsibility, as some of the contestants (such as Ereka and Heidi, who seemed to want other people to make the tough decisions while they took the credit) were not, then you're probably not cut out to be a leader.

And if you plan to delegate an important decision, it is always wise to delegate it to an individual rather than to a group. There's nothing wrong with giving someone access to the resources of a team or group, but it's just about impossible to hold a group responsible for success. It's considerably easier to hold a single person responsible.

Leaders don't shy away from making choices. This is not to say that analysis and research are unnecessary, but rather that those who wish to rise to the top must always be willing to draw the final conclusions. If that means rejecting consensus, so be it.

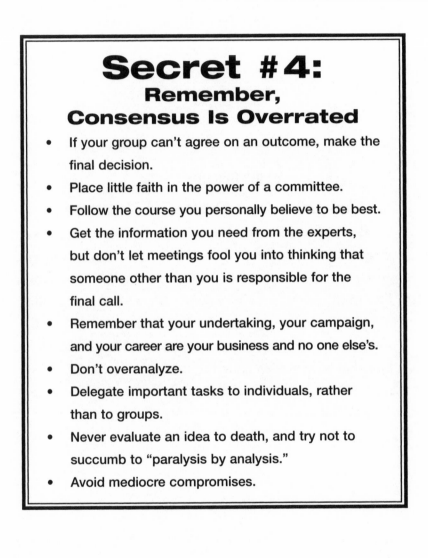

Secret #4:
Remember,
Consensus Is Overrated

- If your group can't agree on an outcome, make the final decision.
- Place little faith in the power of a committee.
- Follow the course you personally believe to be best.
- Get the information you need from the experts, but don't let meetings fool you into thinking that someone other than you is responsible for the final call.
- Remember that your undertaking, your campaign, and your career are your business and no one else's.
- Don't overanalyze.
- Delegate important tasks to individuals, rather than to groups.
- Never evaluate an idea to death, and try not to succumb to "paralysis by analysis."
- Avoid mediocre compromises.

AN APPRENTICE ASIDE:

Advice for Donald Trump

Between his signature hairstyle and his ostentatious penthouse, it's clear that Trump is not as savvy in some areas as he is in business. Why doesn't he hire the Fab Five from *Queer Eye for the Straight Guy* to make him and his place over? He could probably get a reduced rate or some sort of deal on that, now that NBC owns Bravo. Not that money is an issue for him, of course.

SECRET

#5

Identify All Possible Resources, and Use Them Strategically

It was, perhaps, no coincidence that the person who won the competition in the first season of *The Apprentice*, Bill Rancic, had previously founded his own company: an Internet-driven cigar-of-the-month store that sold to stogie enthusiasts. Rancic launched the online business after college, built it up from scratch, and sold it seven years later for a seven-figure sum.

The person whom the Donald selected in the final round of the show turned out to be someone who possessed real-world experience in an area that all small business owners must master: finding resources and using them intelligently. New businesses that don't identify and exploit non-cash resources quickly die. This is a fact of entrepreneurial life. Entrepreneurs who fail this survival test watch their companies go up in smoke. Those who pass the test—by thinking creatively about all the resources that might possibly be at their disposal—are more likely to light up celebratory Havanas.

Successful entrepreneurs understand that cash is to businesses as blood is to the human body. Granted, you may choose to donate blood to the Red Cross every once in a while, but you'll still want to hold on to as much of it as you possibly can. The same basic principle applies to the green stuff coursing around the veins of your company. You won't survive for long if you spend the day looking for ways to give it away.

Allocating precious dollars is only one way to expend your resources. Spending money should be a last resort—not a first resort. If you ignore all the other resources at your disposal, you will fail. One way or another, people who thrive as entrepreneurs master this principle. People who have spent all of their working lives receiving a paycheck from someone else, on the other hand, may be inclined to believe that all resources have dollar signs attached to them.

There are many, many other ways to solve problems besides throwing money at them. To win in Trump's world, you must be willing to ask yourself: What resources can I tap that have little or nothing to do with writing a check? You will eventually identify many non-cash resources, including your own creativity, your ability to initiate new partnerships, your company's ability to help others achieve their strategic goals, and your customer base.

For example, in one task, the show's contestants had to sell Trump Ice, Trump's brand of bottled drinking water. They could sell it by the case, by the pallet, or by the truckload, but the two teams were having difficulty convincing retailers to purchase large quantities, because most stores and restaurants didn't have enough storage space. When Troy realized that they could sell Trump Ice over time (a certain number of cases per week), rather than all at once, he was using his creativity as a resource. And it worked, solving the storage problem for the customers and persuading them that they could place bigger orders.

The following are some of the results of focusing intelligently on non-cash resources.

Get the things you need without paying full price for them.

What kind of special vendor relationships can you develop? Will any vendor accept in-kind or barter arrangements? Can you help any vendor win public attention that might not otherwise be available, as Kwame did in the lemonade challenge? By convincing a vendor that his team's lemonade stand would attract more potential customers to the area, he obtained free ice, cups, and transportation from the vendor. Can you give vendors access to people who represent good business prospects to them? Can you help vendors who have public-relations problems build a better market image for themselves? Can you borrow, repurpose, trade for, or rescue abandoned materials or components? What can you liberate from the scrap yard, avoid throwing away in the first place, or pick up at a bargain rate at nontraditional outlets (like flea markets or auctions)? While preparing for the flea-market task in episode five, Nick and Katrina found a garment rack in a Dumpster that would be ideal for displaying their homemade women's T-shirts at the market—the perfect example of a free resource.

Attract the notice of likely consumers without paying for advertising. Embarking on expensive, untested advertising and promotional campaigns is a classic mistake. How can you use word of mouth to develop your business? What about cold calling? How can you win referrals from people you already know and/or do business with?

Get people to work for you for free...at least for a while. Are you taking full advantage of family connections? Internship possibilities? Often, young people interested in a particular industry will be eager to gain any experience in it, even if they're not earning a paycheck.

Manage your own time and the time of your company's people more effectively. What can you do to improve your own efficiency? How can you eliminate ineffective working habits within your company? How can you use non-cash resources (like public recognition or an extra day off) to reward people for new ideas about how to operate more intelligently?

Improve your relationship with existing customers. Customers are a critical business resource; we sometimes forget that it is far easier to win a sale from someone we are currently doing business with than it is to win business from a total stranger. Whom can you reach out to within your customer base for new business opportunities? Strategic advice? Help in setting up important new alliances? In the pedicab challenge, the show's two teams had to make as much money as they could with a fleet of pedicabs. Team Versacorp approached some of the businesses they had worked with in earlier tasks and managed to sell them advertising space on the backs of the pedicabs. They certainly had an easier time selling this idea to previous contacts than they would have had selling it to total strangers.

Knowing about these kinds of results will help you make the most of resources you may be neglecting, resources that have nothing to do with bank accounts. Henry Ford turned the shipping crates, in which he received automobile parts, into wooden components of the cars themselves! This is the kind of thinking that allows an executive to succeed, an initiative to thrive, and a business to survive.

To succeed at the highest level of American business, it is

important to revisit one of the critical requirements for success in small business: seeing your time, your relationships, your corporate image, and your willingness to think creatively as resources.

Secret #5:
Identify All Possible Resources, and Use Them Strategically

- Identify and exploit noncash resources.
- Spend money only as a last resort.
- Get supplies you need without paying full price for them whenever possible.
- Look for ways to attract the notice of potential customers without paying for advertising.
- Try to find people who will work for you for free.
- Manage your own time and the time of your employees more effectively.
- Improve your relationships with existing customers.

AN APPRENTICE ASIDE:
The Water Distributor

When the two teams attempted to sell Trump Ice, Trump's brand of bottled drinking water, Nick approached a distributor, ABC Office Essentials, which decided not to buy any cases of water. It turns out that ABC Office Essentials has worked with the world of reality television before, on Rocco DiSpirito's NBC show, *The Restaurant*. It has been suggested on many fan websites that the representative of ABC Office Essentials was being disagreeable to Nick on purpose, just to create good television.

SECRET

#6

Cut Your Losses

If you want truly to understand something,
try to change it.

—Kurt Lewin,
social scientist (1890-1947)

An effective leader must be willing to change what is not working, and to do so without apology.

This means reshuffling the team when it is clear that the team is not delivering the desired results. It means reconfiguring a design or product line when it becomes clear that market tastes have changed. It means dropping a project or initiative that is losing money. And it means firing people when it becomes clear that they are not helping the organization attain key strategic goals.

In the world of Trump, just like on *The Apprentice*, people get fired every week. It may seem harsh to suggest that your organization's success is rooted in the principle of getting rid of people. But is firing someone really all that different from changing your approach to attaining a goal?

And is there anything to be said for retaining the services of someone who is making success more difficult? Or for continuing to pay a person who is negative or who destabilizes the organization?

For example, during the final task on *The Apprentice*, when Kwame was in charge of the Jessica Simpson concert at the Trump Taj Mahal in Atlantic City, Omarosa, who was supposed to be one of Kwame's employees, caused Kwame and his team endless trouble. She lied about problems with Jessica Simpson and her band's transportation to the Taj Mahal, goofed off with the band while she should have been escorting Jessica to a VIP meet-and-greet, and then disappeared with Jessica to the Simpson suite, leaving Kwame and his team with no clue as to her or Jessica's whereabouts. However, Kwame didn't fire Omarosa. In the end, Trump couldn't understand Kwame's reluctance to get rid of someone who was such a liability to his team, and this is one of the reasons Kwame lost the final challenge and didn't become the apprentice.

Not all team members mesh. Not all products connect with consumers. And not all people deserve to stay on the team.

Let's face it. The yardsticks by which today's businesses are judged are markers like profitability, efficiency, and achievement of goals. Human beings are, alas, not necessarily profit-minded, efficient, or goal-oriented creatures. If a person on your team is making a habit of subtracting more than he or she adds to the project, you, as the leader, have an obligation to say "You're fired."

Good reasons to reshuffle a team include:
- an inability to attain realistic, measurable goals
- an unwillingness to compete
- persistent personality problems within the group
- excessive politicking

Good reasons to change a design, approach, or product line include:
- unprofitability
- failure to connect in an exciting way with the target market
- failure to keep up with the competition
- failure to reflect the organization's direction

Good reasons to fire a team member include:
- an unhealthy fixation on gossip or backbiting (not at all the same thing as competitive drive)
- an inability to tell the truth
- an obsession with politicking
- a tendency to blame others for his or her own shortcomings
- an inability to commit to or deliver on the organization's overriding goals
- misuse of scarce resources
- a failure to attain clearly communicated goals

On *The Apprentice,* people were fired and teams were reshuffled for each of the above reasons.

Who besides a leader can carry out the task of changing course in any of these areas? And who besides a leader has the moral obligation to implement the decision?

Sometimes we worry that cutting our losses—whether that means getting rid of someone, reshuffling a team, or building a new approach to doing business—will have negative effects on our company or work group. It is just as important to ask, however, whether it will demoralize the team even more to continue to devote resources, time, and energy to something or someone that is not working.

An effective leader must be willing

to change what is not working, and

to do so without apology.

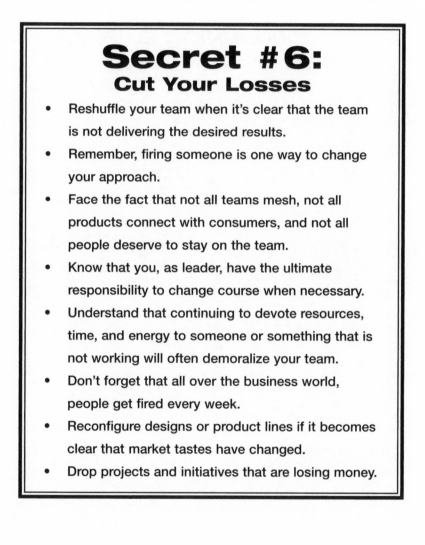

Secret #6:
Cut Your Losses

- Reshuffle your team when it's clear that the team is not delivering the desired results.

- Remember, firing someone is one way to change your approach.

- Face the fact that not all teams mesh, not all products connect with consumers, and not all people deserve to stay on the team.

- Know that you, as leader, have the ultimate responsibility to change course when necessary.

- Understand that continuing to devote resources, time, and energy to someone or something that is not working will often demoralize your team.

- Don't forget that all over the business world, people get fired every week.

- Reconfigure designs or product lines if it becomes clear that market tastes have changed.

- Drop projects and initiatives that are losing money.

AN APPRENTICE ASIDE:
Thoughts on Carolyn

Carolyn, one of Trump's trusted cohorts in the boardroom and an executive at one of Trump's golf courses, is only thirty-five. And, though it shouldn't be relevant, she is extremely attractive. In age, though not in experience, she was a peer to the female contestants on the show. Isn't it interesting to wonder what she made of the show itself, and especially of the female contestants? Do you think she may have resented the fact that they were trying to take shortcuts to attain the type of position that she won through hard work? Might she feel that some of the women's use of sexuality in their attempts to lure customers and clients reinforced stereotypes and has had a negative effect on women in the business world? And considering that Carolyn already has what the contestants wanted, shouldn't they have shown her a bit more respect, instead of complaining about her—as Ereka, Heidi, and Omarosa did—in their exit interviews?

SECRET

#7

Get Face-to-Face with Key Decision Makers

Every wall is a door.

—Ralph Waldo Emerson

When in doubt, go to the top. And when possible, do it in person.

In Trump's world, there is no substitute for one-on-one interaction with key people.

If you're trying to win over a new customer, do whatever you have to do in order to get eye-to-eye with that person, and then make your case with passion and style. If you've been handed an opportunity to develop a new initiative for a client or customer, set up a meeting so you can confirm the goals you'll be trying to attain, and so you can get feedback on your strategies for reaching those goals. If you've inherited (or caused) a problem with an important person or group, ask for a chance to defend yourself and your team—in person—and then chart a new direction.

Too much of today's business communication takes place remotely, behind the technological barrier of faxes, e-mail, voice mail, and videoconferencing. There's nothing wrong with these tools in and of themselves, of course, but when it comes to laying the foundation for an important business relationship, making the most of a unique opportunity, or correcting a potentially destructive error, there's nothing like face-to-face interaction.

You'll notice that this secret includes two important terms: *face-to-face* and *key decision-maker*. Both are essential for success, and both deserve your attention.

Getting face-to-face means giving yourself the chance to read and interpret the body language, facial expressions, and unspoken "comments" that another person displays during your presentation. Effective executives know full well that these elements of communication are just as important—if not more important—as the words spoken during the course of a meeting.

Getting face-to-face also means giving yourself the opportunity to bond with the other person as an individual. If you don't, you won't be able to get a direct feeling for your contact's distinctive way of interacting with the world, for his or her unique goals, and for the way he or she reaches decisions and picks allies. If this is the case, you will in all likelihood find yourself at a competitive disadvantage.

If you choose not to invest your time, money, and energy in a face-to-face meeting with your organization's key decision-makers, both internal and external, you may rest assured that your competition will be ready to make that investment.

When the Versacorp team was planning the ad for the Marquis Jet Card in the second episode, they decided that meeting with the client was unnecessary, while the women of Team Protégé thought it was important to meet the client to get a better understanding of their expectations and desires. By meeting with the important decision-makers—the clients—Team Protégé developed a campaign that better suited their needs. The women went on to win this particular challenge, so it's obvious which team chose the best approach!

A key decision-maker is a person who has the influence, experience, and authority to get things done. As he said on the show, Trump focuses on personal interaction with the "movers and shakers," not with those who report to them. If at first you don't succeed in your efforts to connect personally with the man or woman who has the capacity to give you what you want, think creatively and try a new approach.

But don't be fooled by appearances. If you aspire to a leadership role, it makes no sense whatsoever to commit critical resources—such as time, money, effort, and attention—to meetings with midlevel or low-level contacts. Yet there are plenty of salespeople and senior executives who spend most of their business days "fact-finding" with people who have no authority in their organizations. Then they wonder why it takes those organizations so long to take action.

Forget about investing your time with underlings. Do your level best to win in-person attention from the most important players. Listen to their concerns and interpretations of the situation. Then take action in a way that convinces them that meeting with you was—and is—a good business move.

If you choose not to invest your time, money, and energy in a face-to-face meeting with your organization's key decision makers, both internal and external, you may rest assured that your competition will be ready to make that investment.

Secret #7:
Get Face-to-Face with Key Decision-Makers

- When in doubt, go to the top.

- Do whatever you must to get eye-to-eye contact with new customers.

- Make your case with passion and style.

- Understand that nonverbal communication is just as important—if not more important—than words spoken during a meeting.

- If at first you don't succeed in your efforts to connect personally with a key decision-maker, think creatively and try a new approach.

- Don't be fooled by appearances.

- Forget about investing your time with underlings.

- Set up meetings with new customers or clients so you can confirm the goals you'll be trying to attain.

- Always try to get feedback on your strategies.

- If you've caused an important problem, don't be afraid to chart a new direction.

AN APPRENTICE ASIDE:
The Marquis Jet
Advertising Campaign

In the second episode, each team had to design an ad campaign for the Marquis Jet Card, which would offer a certain number of hours of private jet service. The men of Versacorp designed a traditional, conservative ad. The women of Team Protégé created a shocking campaign that included lots of sexual imagery, and they won the challenge.

After the episode aired, a representative of Marquis Jet was interviewed, and said the ad was not something they would ever actually use.

SECRET

#8

Step Up—
Take Intelligent
Chances, and
Then Take
Responsibility

Necessity is the mother of taking chances.
—*Mark Twain*

In the world of Trump, "risk" is not a dirty word. Claiming "My team didn't warn me about the downside," on the other hand, will get your mouth washed out with soap.

People who achieve at the highest levels know full well that taking chances is an essential prerequisite to success. They also know that failures—or, to use the more acceptable term, "temporary setbacks"—come with the territory if you plan to occupy the corner suite someday. The trick is not to avoid taking chances altogether, but to selectively choose the correct risks, the ones that present the best opportunities for you as an individual and for the organization.

One of the jobs of the leader, in the Trump model, is to pick the right risks to take. What does such a risk look like? The right risk has some of the following characteristics:

- It presents the possibility of a high payoff. Does the risk allow you to enjoy significant benefits if you win? Is it, in other words, in keeping with Secret #1: Think Big? If you're going to take the chance of failing, you should have a reason to celebrate big-time if you succeed.

- It has a manageable downside. What's the worst that can happen? If the risk puts your business, your key people, or your reputation in serious jeopardy, it is not worth taking.

- It takes advantage of your demonstrated strengths and resources. Do you and/or your organization have a unique "fit" with this opportunity? Does taking this risk allow you to take advantage of proven competencies and competitive advantages? Take a good, long look at your resources before you answer this important question—and remember that not all of your resources show up in a bank account (see Secret #5).

- It neutralizes the competition. Does taking this chance present you with the opportunity to deal a serious blow to the competition? If the answer is yes, that's a very good sign.

If you are certain that the risk you are considering meets all four of these criteria, then you may rest assured that Trump would approve of the choice to throw the dice. Pick them up off the table, put them in the little cup, shake vigorously, and let them fly. Something interesting is bound to happen. The only question is: What?

No one rolls a seven every time out. And the odds are good that nobody who is in a position to evaluate your performance really expects you to win every time. (Anyone who actually expects a 100 percent frequency of success is sadly divorced from reality, but intelligent people have been known to pretend to expect constant miracles from risk-takers, possibly because it's more entertaining to do so than to always accept the undeniable reality that people sometimes lose their bets, or possibly because it pushes the risk-takers to produce even more.) During the art task on *The Apprentice*, Kwame's team, Team Protégé, took a big risk in choosing Meghan as their artist. They had to host a gallery showing and sell her pieces, which were more difficult and less immediately appealing than some of the other artists'. However, Meghan had an established customer base, and her pieces generally sold for higher prices than the other artists', so Kwame and his team took a calculated risk: They figured that they might sell fewer pieces, but they'd be guaranteed customers, and that the pieces they did sell would bring them more money. This risk failed, and they made less than Team Versacorp did selling more accessible paintings. However, Trump respected Kwame's risk, even though it didn't work out, and Kwame wasn't fired.

If your bet pays off, you're a hero. If your bet doesn't pay off, you're still a hero, at least potentially. Why? Because you selected a smart risk. Even in defeat, you're willing to step up and take responsibility for having had the guts to pick up the dice in the first place. Companies need intelligent, accountable risk-takers, and by identifying yourself as one without hesitation or double-talk, you can position yourself for another roll of the dice later.

Did you notice that one of the things that reliably got people in trouble on *The Apprentice* was their unwillingness to accept responsibility for the results of their team, and their unwillingness to embrace the responsibilities that accompany acceptance of a leadership role? And did you notice how many people who did accept that responsibility got tongue-lashings for making mistakes at the helm, but got to stick around to compete for another week?

One of the reasons Omarosa provoked such hatred among the other contestants and the audience of *The Apprentice* was that she never took responsibility for her mistakes. Even when Carolyn, Trump's associate and colleague in the boardroom, pointed out Omarosa's mispronunciation of Isaac Mizrahi's last name, which Omarosa had badly misspoken during her attempt to negotiate with him for something to auction off at the AIDS benefit, Omarosa wouldn't admit that it was an important error. When she lied to Kwame during the final challenge about the whereabouts of Jessica Simpson, she wouldn't admit her mistake, even though cameras had obviously captured it.

Troy, on the other hand, was always quick to admit his faults, as well as to share the praise for his achievements, and this ensured that he stayed on the show longer than Omarosa did. When the teams were trying to sell Trump Ice bottled drinking water to various New York businesses and distributors, Troy was the real deal-closer, making the best, most profitable, and most innovative deals for his team. But when he was praised for his achievement, he carefully redistributed the credit between himself and the other members of his team. And when, in a later challenge, his team lost by failing to make enough money with a fleet of pedicabs, he, as project manager, took all the responsibility. This type of behavior impressed Carolyn and Trump in the boardroom.

It just goes to show that it's extremely important to take responsibility for your business decisions. Passing the blame to others just makes you look bad in the eyes of your superiors.

Secret #8:
Step Up—Take Intelligent Chances, and Then Take Responsibility

- Know that failures come with the territory.
- Pick the right risks—the ones that present the possibility of a high payoff, have manageable downsides, take advantage of your demonstrated strengths and resources, and neutralize your competition.
- Take responsibility for your failures.
- Remember that companies need intelligent, accountable risk-takers.
- Don't pass the blame on to others—it just makes you look bad.
- "Risk" is not a dirty word, so don't be afraid to use it.
- Take chances, because they are an essential prerequisite to success.

AN APPRENTICE ASIDE:
The Prizes

The biggest suggestion for the next season, from fans all across the country, is that Trump should offer better prizes for the winning teams. The rewards *were* particularly Trump-centric, but when you look at the list, they really weren't that great, considering what they could have been!

THE PRIZES:

- a tour of Trump's apartment
- a day of golf at one of Trump's golf courses
- a trip to Yankee Stadium to meet George Steinbrenner
- a picnic at Trump's country home
- a helicopter ride above New York City
- ten minutes alone with Trump
- lunch in Palm Beach
- a yacht trip around the city
- $1,000 per person for a night of gambling in Atlantic City (by far the best prize)

SECRET

9

Advance the Most
Profitable Deal

> ***Adventure upon all the tickets in the lottery,
> and you lose for certain; and the greater the
> number of your tickets the nearer your
> approach to this certainty.***
>
> —*Adam Smith*

Some people get a visceral charge out of closing the deal. Trump presumably gets a visceral charge out of closing the *right* deal.

In any business situation, we have only a certain amount of time with which to work. (Time, you will recall, is one of the critical resources we discussed in Secret #5.) Whether we're selling lemonade, running a restaurant for a day, setting up a flea-market booth, negotiating for the resources we need to run our business, or renting event space in Midtown Manhattan, the clock is ticking. Some transactions will dramatically improve our competitive position by promoting our own interests and the interests of our company; other transactions will hardly be worth the trouble of completing. Learning to tell the first kind of deal from the second is a matter of experience, of course, but the sooner you gain that experience, the more likely you are to emerge as a key player within your organization.

In Trump's cutthroat business world, there simply aren't enough hours in the day to justify spending large amounts of time and energy on low-margin deals and product lines. We must constantly promote the transactions that are likely to perform well for us, and in order to do that, we must know ahead of time which deals, of all the potential deals before us, are the most profitable.

This is why, on the show, Amy was so shocked when Omarosa kept offering potential customers small numbers of cases, or even just one case, of Trump Ice, the bottled spring water the teams were selling to area businesses. Considering that the taxi to the meeting probably cost Amy and Omarosa more money than the profit from a single case of water, combined with the amount of time the two women spent trying to close the deal, the fifteen dollars received from the sale of one case obviously wasn't a profitable use of their time. Omarosa should have waited for Amy to try talking the potential clients into purchasing a larger number of cases.

The rule is pretty simple: Invest resources in the most profitable deals, and don't invest resources in deals you know are unlikely to deliver the return or margin you need.

Note that the idea is not merely walking away from unprofitable deals—it should go without saying that you wouldn't risk your own career or the welfare of your team by investing resources in opportunities that drain more than they contribute. The key is to identify business propositions that, though they *do* contribute a small amount, can't realistically be expected to deliver a certain minimum level of performance. It is the task of the leader to establish those minimum requirements, and to make intelligent choices about which deals and offerings are worthwhile in the first place.

There is more—much more—to following through on Secret #9 than simply jacking up your prices and throwing around words like "value" and "brand." Remember the very first challenge the contestants faced during the first season of *The Apprentice*? The task was to sell lemonade to thirsty New Yorkers. The winning team, Team Protégé, charged a premium, but still realistic, price for a glass of lemonade. Team Versacorp, on the other hand, wasted time and resources on a number of low-value ideas. Among the most disastrous of these was their effort to convince upscale New York pedestrians to pay a thousand dollars for a single glass of lemonade. No amount of spin could change the uncomfortable fact that the second team mismanaged their resources. They invested time and energy in a product offering that had a target market so narrow that it was virtually unmeasurable and, in actual practice, totally unattainable.

Advancing the right deal means aggressively—and, yes, stylishly—promoting a carefully considered value proposition, one that needs to make sense to a certain predetermined segment of your market.

Consider the flea-market task. Team Versacorp decided to buy plain women's shirts in bulk, then decorate them with ribbons and other extras. By doing this, they chose a specific market—women—and they could cater to that specific market. Team Protégé, on the other hand, couldn't decide who their customer base was, and they ended up selling a wide variety of random items that didn't strongly appeal to any one market. This is one reason Team Protégé lost this particular challenge.

Advancing the right deal means being willing to inject your own personality and your personal commitment to your business into a certain kind of agreement—an agreement that effectively promotes both your interests and those of your customer or client. For example, when Team Versacorp sold ad space on the back of their pedicabs during the pedicab task, it benefited both their team (by earning them more money on their fleet of pedicabs) and their clients (who obtained advertising space).

Advancing the right deal doesn't mean proposing a deal that generates a tiny return in exchange for the right to call someone your customer, such as Omarosa did when offering to sell extremely small quantities of Trump Ice.

Advancing the right deal doesn't mean demanding a price that insults the intelligence of the person with whom you are trying to do business, and then sitting back and waiting for the money to roll in, as Sam did when he tried to sell a glass of lemonade for one thousand dollars.

Remember, not all deals are equal, and in order to really make an impact on your organization, you have to pursue the right ones.

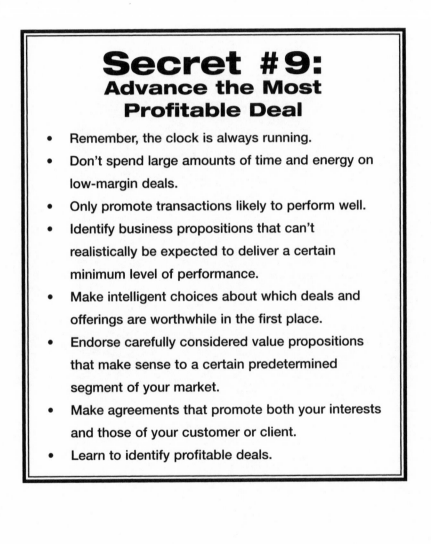

Secret #9:
Advance the Most Profitable Deal

- Remember, the clock is always running.
- Don't spend large amounts of time and energy on low-margin deals.
- Only promote transactions likely to perform well.
- Identify business propositions that can't realistically be expected to deliver a certain minimum level of performance.
- Make intelligent choices about which deals and offerings are worthwhile in the first place.
- Endorse carefully considered value propositions that make sense to a certain predetermined segment of your market.
- Make agreements that promote both your interests and those of your customer or client.
- Learn to identify profitable deals.

AN APPRENTICE ASIDE:
The Deutsch Advertising Time Warp

Before the advertising task really kicked off, Donny Deutsch gave the contestants a tour of Deutsch Advertising. He stressed to Trump and his followers that Deutsch Inc. was an extremely free and open workplace, and, at that very moment, an employee zoomed past on a scooter.

Sounds like fun, sure. But isn't that whole office style a bit too 1995? Do you think they play Nerf ball in the hallways, too?

SECRET #10

Negotiate Tough;

Negotiate Based on Your Negiotiating Partner's Situation and Personality; Understand That No Single Negotiating Strategy is Perfect

You need to have a walk away...
a combination of price, terms, and deliverables
that represents the least you will accept.
Without one, you have no negotiating road map.
—*Keiser*

E very negotiating situation is unique. Anyone who tells you otherwise is probably trying to outnegotiate you.

Once you accept that premise, you'll understand that there really is no single negotiating principle—no simple, catchy precept that will see you through all the steps that compose the intricate dance we call closing a deal.

Experience, instinct, and the ability to read others accurately are essential components of any successful negotiating session. There are, however, three basic principles you should bear in mind while learning to negotiate effectively on behalf of your organization and yourself. These principles are the subject of this chapter; they are offered not as the last word, but as the beginning of a long-term process that will help you expand your own skills.

Ask the advice of others in your organization, learn from past negotiating sessions, and use the following principles as starting points. With a little practice, you will eventually master the skill of negotiating the deal, as practiced all over the business world.

Negotiate tough. This means knowing when to walk away. You also must be able to broadcast your willingness to walk away if you don't get the right deal, and then actually walk away if the circumstances require that you do so. Negotiating tough is not something that comes naturally. It takes effort to identify the point at which it makes the most sense for you to disengage from a negotiating session, and it takes practice to learn how to use the prospect of your departure as an incentive that will motivate the other side.

Negotiate based on your negotiating partner's situation and personality style. You really do have to adapt your strategy, and your speaking style, to the person you're talking to. What works spectacularly in one negotiation can fail just as spectacularly when you try it with a different person. Keep in mind that different people are motivated by different things: Some people are motivated by the need to prove to others that they've secured important concessions; other people are motivated by the desire to display their technical knowledge; other people are motivated by the need to keep their businesses afloat. And quite a few people are motivated by the desire for power. The ability to deal with the various situations and personality types is a matter of experience; it can't be taught overnight. You can, however, begin to get a sense of what you're up against if you ask clarifying questions when you're presented with an offer or counteroffer such as, "How did you arrive at that figure?"

When Team Protégé was trying to negotiate celebrity events to auction off at the Elizabeth Glaser Pediatric AIDS Foundation benefit, Russell Simmons (a major figure in the hip-hop world) didn't respond well to Kwame's formal negotiating, or to Omarosa's efforts to ingratiate herself to him. But he responded immediately to Troy's easygoing manner. Troy's comfortable negotiating style, however, may not have worked as well on a different type of person. You should always be ready to change your demeanor, from one negotiating partner to the next. Troy's charming, "give in because everyone wins" negotiating attitude worked wonderfully in fun situations, such as the charity auction, but not as well in serious ones, when people were more wary of being hustled. This is why he had a difficult time convincing people to rent the Trump Tower penthouse space for an event.

Understand that no single negotiating strategy is perfect. If you don't have a good sense of the personality or agenda of your negotiating partner, you may have to try several different approaches before a meaningful discussion gets under way.

Any amount of research you can do beforehand is always helpful. During the third episode of *The Apprentice*, when

Amy negotiated to buy a golf club, she offered "cost plus ten percent" and quoted the figure—three hundred dollars— showing she had researched the price of the club. This helped her get the deal she wanted. In a later episode, when Team Protégé was going to meet with the Fab Five from *Queer Eye for the Straight Guy* to enlist their participation in the Elizabeth Glaser Pediatric AIDS Foundation benefit, Troy removed his belt, knowing that this fashion faux pas would endear the Fab Five to him. This little piece of advance preparation worked spectacularly, and the Fab Five agreed to auction off an evening of Gay Disco Bowling, which brought in $9,000 for the foundation.

Compare these situations to the water-selling task, in which Nick tried to sell Trump Ice to ABC Office Essentials without doing his homework. He hadn't researched the company beforehand, which presumably factored into his inability to secure a deal with the distributor.

Even though you should be willing to try different strategies, there are certain basic principles that will hold true in every negotiation. For instance: Whenever possible, negotiate face-to-face (see Secret #7). Never give something up without getting something in return (see Secret #2). And, last but not least, never be afraid to ask for something big (see Secret #1). After all, that's the Trump way.

There really is no single negotiating

principle—no simple, catchy precept

that will see you through all the

steps that compose the intricate

dance we call closing a deal.

Secret #10:
Negotiate Tough; Negotiate Based on Your Negotiating Partner's Situation and Personality; Understand That No Single Negotiating Strategy Is Perfect

- Remember, every negotiating situation is unique.
- Ask the advice of others with experience before a negotiation.
- Learn from past negotiation sessions.
- Know when to walk away.
- Adapt your strategy to the person you're talking to.
- Keep in mind that different people are motivated by different things.
- Research beforehand.
- Never be afraid to ask for something big.

THE TEN SECRETS BLUEPRINT

SECRET #1: THINK BIG

Learning to focus on extra-large goals isn't just a temporary expedient. It's the way some people train themselves to live their lives and to get past obstacles that make small-thinking colleagues shudder. It may be possible to succeed in the business world by focusing obsessively on small, incremental ideas, or by methodically refining a series of low-level initiatives. It's fair to say, though, that you're unlikely to impress Donald Trump (or any number of similar people) by working this way.

SECRET #2: SHOW THE COMPETITION NO MERCY

In the world of the high achiever, competition is a rule of life. The aim is to win, by outperforming other teams and your own teammates: to win fairly and to play by the rules, but to come in first without apologizing for wanting to do so. In order to win, you have to be willing to outwork, out think, out-promote, and outmaneuver the competition.

SECRET #3: DEFEND YOURSELF AGGRESSIVELY

Don't waste precious time complaining that an attack was not fair and then expecting others to take up your defense. Don't waste precious time wishing you had anticipated the nature or direction of the attack. Don't waste precious time celebrating the defense you had planned against a different attack you thought you would face but did not. Deal with this attack. Leaders must come to grips with the fact that attacks come from all sides. Leaders know that they cannot possibly expect to anticipate the specifics of every attack. Failing to predict an attack is not a mistake. The mistake is expecting attacks to diminish or disappear by letting them go unanswered.

SECRET #4: REMEMBER, CONSENSUS IS OVERRATED

Leaders don't shy away from making choices. This is not to say that analysis and research are unnecessary, but rather that those who wish to rise to the top must always be willing to draw the final conclusions. If that means rejecting consensus, so be it.

SECRET #5: IDENTIFY ALL POSSIBLE RESOURCES, AND USE THEM STRATEGICALLY

Henry Ford turned shipping crates, in which he received automobile parts, into wooden components of the cars themselves. This is the kind of thinking that allows an executive to succeed, an initiative to thrive, and a business to survive. Always remember the non-monetary resources—such as time, creativity, and contacts—that you have at your disposal.

SECRET #6: CUT YOUR LOSSES

Sometimes we worry that cutting our losses—whether that means firing someone, reshuffling a team, or building a new approach to doing business—will have negative effects on our company or work group. It is just as important to ask, however, whether continuing to devote resources, time, and energy to something or someone that is not contributing enough might demoralize the team even more.

SECRET #7: GET FACE-TO-FACE WITH KEY DECISION MAKERS

Forget about investing your time in fact-finding sessions with underlings. Do your best to win in-person attention from the most important players, the people who have authority and influence. Listen to their concerns and interpretations of the situation. Then take action in a way that convinces them that meeting with you was—and is—a good business move.

SECRET #8: STEP UP—TAKE INTELLIGENT CHANCES, AND THEN TAKE RESPONSIBILITY

People who achieve at the highest levels know full well that taking chances is an essential prerequisite to success. They also know that failures—or, to use the more acceptable term, "temporary setbacks"—come with the territory if you plan to occupy the corner suite someday. The trick is not to avoid taking chances altogether, but to selectively choose the correct risks, the ones that present the best opportunities for you as an individual and for the organization as a whole. Once you throw the dice, take full responsibility for having done so.

SECRET #9: ADVANCE THE MOST PROFITABLE DEAL

In the world of Trump, there simply aren't enough hours in the day to justify spending large amounts of time and energy on low-margin deals and product lines. You must constantly promote the transactions that are likely to perform best. In order to do that, you must know ahead of time which deals, of all the potential deals before you, are the most profitable.

SECRET #10: NEGOTIATE TOUGH; NEGOTIATE BASED ON YOUR NEGOTIATING PARTNER'S SITUATION AND PERSONALITY; UNDERSTAND THAT NO SINGLE NEGOTIATING STRATEGY IS PERFECT

Experience, instinct, and the ability to read others accurately are essential components of any successful negotiating session. There are, however, three basic principles you should bear in mind while learning to negotiate effectively on behalf of your organization and yourself. Use them!

BONUS SECRET #1: DRESSING FOR SUCCESS

Sometimes, success is in the eye of the beholder. Dressing well will never guarantee you the next job, though you should wear a good suit to your next interview. But dressing badly can sometimes tarnish people's opinions of you. People are superficial, or no one would be watching half the programming on network television. But wardrobe will never completely take the place of hard work and accomplishment.

No matter whether you are a man or a woman, how you dress says a lot about you. It says a lot about your ambitions, about how you view yourself, and how you view your job. The first advice is to always dress as well as your boss. Don't try to outdress your boss. Do not buy more expensive suits or outfits. Do not buy more expensive shoes, shirts, blouses, ties, etc. Don't show off your new wardrobe. Simply, if your boss wears a suit everyday, then you wear a suit everyday. If he wears a tie, and you're a man, you wear a tie. If your boss is a bad dresser, then dress better but don't flaunt it. Dressing well is about presenting an image to the rest of the people you work with. It says something to clients and potential clients, as well as to potential employers.

Dressing well isn't about wearing labels. Cary Grant and Fred Astaire dressed well, but neither ever wore Polo, or Calvin Klein, or any other label on their chest. Neither did Greta Garbo or Katherine Hepburn. And dressing well doesn't mean you have to spend lot of money. We're talking about style. We're talking about keeping it simple.

BASIC RULES FOR MEN AND WOMEN

The best basic rule is this: **KEEP YOUR ATTIRE SIMPLE, CLEAN, AND PRESSED**. Believe it or not, Donald Trump and Cary Grant had something in common: their fashion sense. No, we're not crazy. Seriously, if you ever look at Cary Grant, publicity stills or movie stills, he dressed simply— solid suits, soild shirts, and solid ties. So does Trump. It cuts a clean, classic figure, with nice lines, and it keeps the Fashion Victim factor to a minimum. That's the real secret to dressing for executive success.

Many people are always trying to wear the latest thing. That's not a good idea. Have you ever seen a picture of yourself five years after you've worn the latest thing? Oh, you burned that picture? That's why the best advice is to avoid those outfits and accessories too.

Suits and Sport Coats – The best colors are blues, grays, and black. Tans, greens, and browns are nice for change of pace, but should not be the mainstay of your wardrobe.

Ties and Scarves – Solid colors are always best. Don't try to be a trend setter. In the fall wear maroon, navy, black, gray, gold, chocolate brown, forest green, and cream colored ties and scarves. In the summer wear yellows, pinks, bright reds, and blues. If you desire patterns, keep them clean, neat, and simple. Polka-dots are nice. Stripes are always a good bet. Try not to complicate the colors.

Socks and Stockings – Socks should always match your pants (or stockings) and your shoes, whichever is darker. If you are wearing a tan suit and dark brown shoes, you wear dark socks. If you are wearing tan pants and white shoes, socks or stockings should match your pants as well. In executive dress, the darker the stockings, the better.

Shirts and Blouses – Solids are your best bet and should compose the largest portion of your dress wardrobe. Blouses and shirts that are patterned should make up no more than 25% of your collection. With patterned shirts you should not stray far from basic stripes—blues and grays are best. Monotone guncheck patterns are nice in the fall, and simple ginghams are nice in the spring.

Shoes – The simpler the better. For men a basic pair of

lace-up black, lace-up brown, and a pair of simple brown or oxblood slip-on loafers are all that's needed. For women, the same dictum applies. Women especially tend to fall fashion victim here, more than anywhere else.

Cuff links – French cuff shits are very nice accessories. Men who buy French cuff shirts show class and sophistication. But again, keep the colors solid and the collars plain. Buy nice cuff links, but keep them moderate in size. This is certainly a place where you can have some fun, but in the end a simple pair of gold knots will be the best investment you ever make. Large, showy cuff links make you look like an escapee from the *Goodfellas* set.

Earrings – Nice earrings are always the capper to a smart, sophisticated look. But how many times have you seen crazy earrings make a woman look like a bad Christmas tree decorated by kindergarteners? A simple pair of pearl, diamond, or zarconia studs, and some simple gold knots or small hoops, are all you really need.

Dresses – Simples rules still apply. The hemline should not be more higher than just above the knee, and the neck line should not show any cleavage. Are we going out to dinner or going to work?

CASUAL FRIDAYS

This is where you can tell the boys and girls from the men and women. Men and women dress nicely on casual Fridays, and boys and girls dress like they are going to a cookout. A few helpful hints: All your clothes should be neatly ironed. No one wants to look at the clothes you keep wrinkled up in a ball all week, even if it is a Friday. No T-shirts in the office! No sweat pants! No shorts! And no sneakers!

A pair of nicely pressed khakis and a button-down shirt or polo shirt will do nicely for men. Women have a wide array of casual choices, but make sure to keep it flattering, simple, and pressed.

POSTURE!

Yes, posture is a part of dressing! Don't slouch. It will give you a bad back and it makes you look lazy and stupid. This is one time we're going to agree with your mother.

MEN - DO'S AND DON'TS

- Do wear a solid white or blue shirt with a pinstripe suit of any kind
- Do wear a solid colored shirt with a patterned suit or sport coat
- Do wear a patterned or striped shirt with a solid suit
- Do have your eyebrows trimmed
- Do wear an aftershave or cologne, but keep it subtle
- Do keep breath mints available at all times

- Do not wear jeans on casual Fridays
- Do not wear loafers with a suit
- Do not let chest hair crawl up over your shirt collar

- Do not wear ties decorated with flowers, comic book characters, or any licensed logos

WOMEN - DO'S AND DON'TS

- Do wear a nice cologne or other fragrance, but keep it subtle
- Do wear simple flats or heels that are comfortable and not too high
- Do wear solid colored dresses and suits
- Do wear simple, clean styles of suits and dresses
- Do keep breath mints available at all times

- Do not wear miniskirts
- Do not show your mid-riff
- Do not apply make-up at your desk
- Do not brush your hair at your desk
- Do not do your nails at your desk
- Do not wear plunging neck lines
- Do not wear pumps to the office
- Do not wear jeans on casual Fridays
- Do not wear fishnets to work

BONUS SECRET #2: SUCCESSFUL EXECUTIVE ETIQUETTE

"Your manners are always under examination, and by committees little suspected, awarding or denying you very high prizes when you least think it."

—Ralph Waldo Emerson

FIRST IMPRESSIONS COUNT

According to the University of California, Santa Barbara, Counseling and Career Services, "The First 12 Words you speak should include some form of thanks if appropriate. When meeting someone for the first time, express your gratitude. Examples: Thank you for scheduling this meeting (or) It is a pleasure meeting you (or) I appreciate the time you have taken to arrange for us to meet."

That's about as simple and direct as we can make it. Be confident. Don't be loud or obnoxious, but rather be warm, friendly, and professional.

RULES OF INTRODUCTION

Introductions are the most important part of any business experience. From the interview to meeting with co-workers, from wooing prospective clients to meeting with current clients, the introduction is always key. The University of California put the keys to successful introductions in the follow order, and we agree:

Stand up.

Smile.

Always shake hands, and firmly.

Make eye contact.

Repeat the other person's name.

THE NORMAL RULES OF ETIQUETTE APPLY — ONLY MORE SO

Opening office doors, conference room doors, and car doors never goes out of style. Saying *excuse me*, and not using foul language, never goes out of style either. These are the first etiquette rules of successful executives. More successful individuals foul up here than anywhere else. Manners can make the difference between getting the account, the sale, or the job. Don't blow it!

There are countless careers that have hit the rocks because someone exhibited bad or rude behavior in a setting where it was inappropriate. Manners matter more at work than anywhere. If you were a high-ranking official and you wanted to hand over a job worth more than $100,000, would you hand it over to someone who was slovenly or rude? Doubtful. When we act rudely, we give the impression that we are either unaware, uneducated, or that we just don't care.

Table manners are also important. Make sure to place your napkin on your lap. Remember to wipe your mouth with your napkin from time to time. Do not guzzle your beverage. Do not burp at the table. Do not reach across the table. Remember to say things like, "Please pass the salt" and "Thank you." And remember that politics and religion are off-limit subjects, especially at client lunches.

- Do not tell lewd jokes.
- Do not use foul language.
- Do not talk about sex or use innuendo.
- Do not take clients to inappropriate establishments.
- Do not giggle.
- Do not touch. A handshake is fine, anything else might be misconstrued.

SUCCESSFUL MINGLING

This admittedly can be the hardest part of the job, but it can also be the most rewarding. There is nothing so dull as a guest who doesn't mingle. People who are forgotten because they didn't meet anyone, are unlikely to be invited again. If you arrive at a get-together and realize that you don't know anyone, be honest, be up-front, and be the first to say hello.

"When approaching a group of people whose body language appears to be open to having others join them, say 'I don't know anyone here, and wanted to introduce myself. My name is_____.' Most polished professionals who understand what it's like to enter a room filled with unfamiliar faces will welcome you into their group—at least for a few minutes," states the University of California.

It's always a good idea to approach individuals who are standing alone. In most cases they are feeling just as awkward as you are, and will be grateful for the opportunity. If the person seems uninterested, be polite, step out of the conversation, and approach someone new.

One of the keys to meeting people is to make them feel important. Let them tell you all about themselves. Don't try to compare notes or experiences, because this sometimes offends people. Most people love to talk about themselves, and will, in the end, think of you as a very interesting person because you let them talk to you for so long.

- Do ask if there is anything you can do to help.
- Do offer a hand toward the end of the evening.
- Do make sure to say thank you to the host at least once during the affair.
- Do listen more than you speak.
- Do bring business cards.

- Do not be the last to leave.

- Do not stand by the bar all night.
- Do not stand by the food table all night.
- Do not eat or drink too much.
- Do not invade other people's personal space. Stay an arm's length away.

BONUS SECRET #3: SPEAKING SUCCESSFULLY

BEING A GOOD CONVERSATIONALIST

Being a good conversationalist is one of the most important aspects of being in business. Any business. And most of the great business executives have what the rest of us call a "gift for gab." But in the end, they are in fact great communicators because whether they say a lot or nothing at all, people *feel* like they are being heard by that executive. Communication is the key.

According to the University of Tampa, maintaining eye contact is crucial. Listening closely is another. Some of the big no-no's are the following subjects, which are off-limits in business conversation: "Your health, or more importantly, your illness. Another's health, or more importantly, his/her illness. Sensitive topics such as abortion, religion, etc.

money, tragedies, gossip and sex."

COMMUNICATING AT THE $100,000 LEVEL

The ability to communicate is one of the most important things an executive has in his or her tool bag. "Be convincing, be eloquent in your speech and be a good communicator. Asking questions and listening to the person answering them is an important part of communication," maintains the University of California

Speaking skills are also important. If you are bashful about speaking in front of large groups, make sure to practice, and know in advance what you are going to say. Make a short outline on a card or piece of paper. And always remember to be yourself.

HAND GESTURES

Please watch what you do with your hands. Hand movement should be used to enhance what you are saying rather than to detract from your presentation. "Tests have shown that hands visible rather than in pockets project a more positive image," says the University of Tampa.

And here are some other tips from the University of Tampa Career Services office:

- Be well informed and be able to talk on a wide range of subjects.
- Be interested in what other people do for a living.
- Stay informed on the major news happenings of the world.

- Be able to flow from one topic to another with ease.
- Gracefully accept any compliments given to you.
- Be sensitive to the timing of when to talk about non-business topics and vice versa.
- Be sure to converse with everyone within the group.
- Be sensitive to shy people within the group.
- Try to avoid awkward silences.
- Be diplomatic in situations where you are too busy to carry on a conversation.

- Do not pretend to be an expert on all topics.
- Do not correct another's grammar or pronunciation in public.
- Do not ask a professional for advice or information at a social function or casual meeting.

$100,000 VOCABULARY

No, we're not asking you to use words you don't know, but perception is reality. There are four-letter words and there are $100,000 vocabularies. Don't use crude language in business settings and make sure to brush up on your vocabulary. The size of the word isn't important, but when you use it is. You should understand financial terms, but don't start talking shop.

There are many excellent books on this subject. Go to your local library or bookstore and find them. Reading a dictionary is not the best way to do it. It is better to read magazines that follow government, world politics, geography, medicine, or another pursuit. Read something other than fashionable magazines and sports pages.

Here are four great vocabulary builder titles worth reading:

30 DAYS TO A MORE POWERFUL VOCABULARY
by Wilfred Funk and Norman Lewis
Paperback, 244 pages
Pocket Books; Reissue edition (March 15, 1991)
ISBN: 067174349X

WORD POWER MADE EASY
by Norman Lewis
Paperback, 528 pages
Pocket Books; Reissue edition (February 15, 1991)
ISBN: 067174190X

MERRIAM-WEBSTER'S VOCABULARY BUILDER
by Mary Wood Cornog
Paperback: 576 pages
Merriam-Webster Mass Market (January 1999)
ISBN: 0877799105

VERBAL ADVANTAGE: TEN EASY STEPS TO A POWERFUL VOCABULARY
by Charles Harrington Elster
Paperback: 496 pages
Publisher: Random House Reference (September 26, 2000)
ISBN: 0375709320

Apprentice Musings by Beth Gottfried

THE AFTERMATH
OF *THE APPRENTICE*:
A PERSONAL ASSESSMENT

Having had the opportunity in recent weeks to distance myself a bit from *The Apprentice*, I've decided that my life has become surprisingly empty. While the show definitely had a major impact on pop culture, it also had a pivotal impact on my career as a columnist, and on my life as a whose. Five months ago I could never have imagined that I would be the co-author of a book based on the show. In fact, initially I tried to squirm my way out of writing an *Apprentice* column in the first place! And now it seems, much like Henry Higgins's fondness for Eliza Doolittle ("I've grown accustomed to her face"), that I've grown attached to the pseudo-real business world of the show, and I scarcely know what to do with myself on Thursday nights now that it's gone. A nervous wreck, I pace the floors of my apartment, wondering how thirteen weeks could have gone by so quickly, and questioning why its abandonment has left me feeling so empty.

I fear that the inevitable has now happened. I've become delusional. The legendary personalities that comprised the first season of the hit show have taken up semi-permanent residence in my brain. They occupy that small space between my ears that used to house air and mindless thoughts.

I no longer have a subconscious of my own.

CASE IN POINT:

- When I think evil thoughts, instead of a devil perching on my shoulder, a single letter hovers there: "O". This can only mean one thing, and I think you and I both know what it is.

- When I feel misunderstood or misrepresented, I immediately think of the whole Ereka/Omarosa debacle. Sticks and stones may break my bones, but words can never hurt me. Um, yeah, about that...

- Whenever I feel guilty about my negative attitude (re: life hasn't given me all that I deserve), I say to myself or aloud (depending on whether or not I have company), "Look at Troy." I remember all the adversity he's faced and the optimism he nonetheless emanates. I'm not worthy to shine his shoes. It reminds me that I should be grateful and appreciate what I have.

• Sometimes I sit on my couch admiring my legs (I'm a runner). Then I think, "Remember Katrina?" Katrina has amazing legs, and gorgeous hair, and a contract with Venus or Gillette. That's why I hate her. Then I try to think of something negative about her, to remember one of the embarrassing things she did on the show, and while it doesn't quite make up for the hair/leg combo, it does makes my present reality a little cheerier. Please refrain from all judgment here.

• Heidi cursed like I've never heard a gal curse before. Subsequently, I swear a lot less now. It got to be a little gratuitous.

• Kwame brings out the intellectual elitist labeling stuff that I wholeheartedly despise. It's like no one can say the man's name without saying "Harvard MBA" in the same, elongated breath. Does anyone know Kwame's last name? No. And why? Because the only thing we hear after his name is the dropping of the H-bomb. And I don't know how I feel about his designation as one of this year's *50 Most Beautiful People*. I mean, you can't have looks and brains. Pick one or the other. There's not enough to go around.

- Bill Rancic is all wrong. He's a mythical Zeus-like figure. He should not have won the car, the dream job, and the beautiful down-to-earth woman all in one night. It was a little too American Dream for me. Leaders and heroes should be people who triumph over a long period time, only after enduring years of isolation, brainwashing, and torture.

Oh well, I suppose I'll survive. Maybe not having *The Apprentice* around will force me to go out and be more social and have a life. And hey, there's always next season.

THE BATTLE OF THE SEXES IN *THE APPRENTICE*

Initially it appeared that the women's team on *The Apprentice*, Team Protégé, would dominate and take Trump's world by storm. In the first few weeks of the show they kicked some serious ass, and it wasn't until the teams were reshuffled that a shift in power and confidence was evident. One by one, the women were systematically eliminated week after week. From their brief position as a powerhouse, they quickly crashed and burned. Even Donald Trump, when interviewed in *Dateline*, didn't know how to respond to this phenomenon. He was just as shocked as the viewers by the demise of the women's dominance. It was almost akin to a social experiment in school, reminiscent of the many theories stating that boys are oftentimes the more aggressive and outspoken of the sexes, and that girls tend to retreat to the back of the class and are much less likely to assert themselves. In any event, the women's supremacy withered and died. It was a sad display. What happened? Was some social or sexual dynamic at play?

I know that we've come a long way since the 1950s, at least partly because the idea of our progress has been continually bashed into my head since I was a teenager. Terms like "glass ceiling" make me cringe. I shudder to think that in the past few decades, women haven't been as recognized or appreciated as men, despite their similar merits and achievements. I shudder to think this, yet I have experienced it firsthand.

What is even more disheartening to me, however, is that as a working woman, my biggest critics are most often other women. In the past, I've received more support and constructive criticism from male coworkers than from female ones. It's in times like these when I think: Where is the solidarity, the sisterhood? Shouldn't we all be rooting for each other? Over the past five years, I have had one male boss and several female bosses. My kindest and most fair-minded boss to date was, in fact, the one man. My first regular job out of college was working for a start-up publishing company where the Managing Editor was a woman. I remember how harshly she judged me and other women and how quick she was to commend the men. I also remember starting at the same time as a male coworker who had the same amount of work experience as I did. It was a crushing blow when I discovered that he earned a starting salary considerably higher than mine, but it also taught me to bargain and negotiate for myself. In the future, I would never again be that naïve. In other words, I learned to do what my mother taught me from the time I was kid—to fight for myself. As she put it, "If you don't fight for yourself, no one else will." She was right.

In truth, my personal experience makes it difficult to watch women on shows like *The Apprentice* use their sexuality to sell. And it's not just *The Apprentice*. We all know it's a tactic that works. It's been proven again and again. However, it's my fear that these antics ultimately lessen the level to which women are taken seriously in the workplace. We've fought so hard to be recognized and appreciated for our contributions, why must we go so far to sell ourselves short? I attended an *Apprentice* party with Ereka and Katrina a few weeks before the show ended, as they were in the process of signing away their physical assets for a myriad of male fans through their controversial *FHM* spread. Ereka was up in arms, spouting about being taken seriously as women. My only thought was—how can we take these women seriously when we see them like that? Why is Kwame showcased in *50 Most Beautiful People*, fully clothed, while these women are baring it all?

I admit that I am somewhat baffled by the feminist movement. I see photos and ads from the '40s like Rosie the

Riveter, and I think about how female strength was aligned with grace, dignity, and form. These days, it's considered to be acceptable for women to expose themselves in overt ways and to flaunt their bodies in the media because they are "expressing" themselves, regardless if this behavior is degrading and demoralizing to their gender. I don't really get this, but perhaps I'm old-fashioned. I know sex sells, but is it essential that we sacrifice our integrity to get ahead? Watching the women of *The Apprentice* would lead one to conclude that sex plays a much bigger role in the business world than it really does. But how much of this is gratuitous and ratings-driven? And how much is actually representative of the real world?

On the other hand, I've been known to wear a hiked-up skirt, form-fitting top, and knee-high boots on occasion (though never all three at once). And when I do, the male attention is there immediately, like a deer in headlights. Does this mean I'm using my body to get ahead? No—at least not on a conscious level.

I had an interesting conversation with a male friend of mine the other day, regarding a female coworker's dress habits. She often wears very tight, unflattering clothing. I see poor fashion choice and a cry for help. He sees a double standard. His concern is how unfair it is that she can get away with wearing such a get-up, when he'd be kicked out of work for wearing such a potentially exposing outfit. While I don't necessarily want to admit it, I suppose he has a point.

Maybe there are a lot of men out there who would like to express themselves more through their clothing, like women do, but aren't allowed the opportunity. But though men rarely (if ever) wear skirts or dresses in Corporate America, I think their standard business casual attire requires a lot less hassle. I think a lot of women would welcome that. Myself included.

So, I guess that as much as we learn from our environment—or, in this case, from a Mark Burnett/Donald Trump collaboration—what shows like this are really presenting is an updated, not always favorable, depiction of the classic battle of the sexes.

PREDICTIONS: WHERE WILL THIS YEAR'S CONTESTANTS END UP?

There is lot of the surreal in reality TV. It's a hyped-up version of the mundane. While I do run into women like Ereka and Katrina from time to time, I have been fortunate enough to avoid most of the Heidis and Omarosas of the world. I know they exist, but I also know that part of the illusion of reality television is the idea that there is a surplus of such personalities in everyday life. My major questions are: a) Are such personalities (the Puck Personas, as I refer to them) somewhat a byproduct of TV? and b) Is there actually a higher percentage of such personality types on reality TV than in the overall population? Having met and formed an acquaintance with one member of the cast, I can say that for the most part, reality show contestants are everyday kinds of people who simply like the attention (even if they would protest that statement). Do they crave it more than average? I'm not so certain. For instance, personally, I love recognition and even attention (to a small degree), but I hate over-exposure and the concept of celebrity.

I think the ability to endure being hooked up to microphone and being taped 24/7 assumes at least a bit of exhibitionism. Of course, reality show contestants are also open to much personal attack and scrutiny. As I told someone I once interviewed, if you sign on to do such a project, you can't have one without the other. It's the price of fame. I do think, however, that different personalities handle fame differently. Someone like Troy may benefit from certain opportunities that wouldn't have otherwise presented themselves (like a free college education) had he not been on television. Other personalities seem to suffer from diva-fixation (the desire to be an actor, celebrity, or all-around diva). In my opinion, it's the dark side of reality TV: giving know-nothings and quacks much more fame, money, and exposure than they ever deserved. This really sends a message that being a b*tch will be rewarded: look at how you can reap benefits from personifying pure evil.

The
$100,000
Resource
Guide

TOP TEN U.S. GRADUATE BUSINESS SCHOOLS

Harvard University
School of Business
Soldiers Field
Boston, MA 02163
(617) 495-6127
Admissions E-mail: admissions@hbs.edu
Web site: http://www.hbs.edu
Electronic application: http://www.hbs.edu/mba/apply/

Stanford University
School of Business
518 Memorial Way
Stanford, CA 94305-5015
(650) 723-2766
Admissions E-mail: mba@gsb.stanford.edu
Web site: http://www.gsb.stanford.edu
Electronic application: http://www.gsb.stanford.edu/apply

University of Pennsylvania (Wharton)
School of Business
420 Jon M. Huntsman Hall, 3730 Walnut Street
Philadelphia, PA 19104
(215) 898-6183
Admissions E-mail: mba.admissions@wharton.upenn.edu

Web site: http://www.wharton.upenn.edu/mba
Electronic application: https://admissions.wharton.upenn.edu/admissions

Massachusetts Institute of Technology (Sloan)
School of Business
50 Memorial Drive
Cambridge, MA 02142
(617) 258-5434
Admissions E-mail: mbaadmissions@sloan.mit.edu
Web site: http://mitsloan.mit.edu/mba
Electronic application: http://mitsloan.mit.edu/mba/admissions/apply.php

Northwestern University (Kellogg)
School of Business
2001 Sheridan Road
Evanston, IL 60208-2001
(847) 491-3308
Admissions E-mail: MBAadmissions@kellogg.northwestern.edu
Web site: http://www.kellogg.northwestern.edu
Electronic application:
http://www.kellogg.northwestern.edu/prospective/index.htm

Columbia University
School of Business
3022 Broadway, 216 Uris Hall
New York, NY 10027
(212) 854-1961
Admissions E-mail: apply@claven.gsb.columbia.edu
Web site: http://www.gsb.columbia.edu
Electronic application: http://www.gsb.columbia.edu/admissions/online

University of Chicago
School of Business
1101 E. 58th Street
Chicago, IL 60637
(773) 702-7369
Admissions E-mail: admissions@gsb.uchicago.edu
Web site: http://gsb.uchicago.edu
Electronic application: http://gsb.uchicago.edu

University of California--Berkeley (Haas)
School of Business
545 Student Services Building
Berkeley, CA 94720-1900
(510) 642-1405
Admissions E-mail: N/A
Web site: http://www.haas.berkeley.edu
Electronic application:
https://ssl.haas.berkeley.edu/admissions/application/

Dartmouth College (Tuck)
School of Business
100 Tuck Hall
Hanover, NH 03755-9000
(603) 646-3162
Admissions E-mail: tuck.admissions@dartmouth.edu
Web site: http://www.tuck.dartmouth.edu
Electronic application: http://app.applyyourself.com/?id=dart-mba

University of Michigan—Ann Arbor
School of Business
701 Tappan Street
Ann Arbor, MI 48109
(734) 763-5796
Admissions E-mail: umbsmba@umich.edu
Web site: http://www.bus.umich.edu
Electronic application: http://www.bus.umich.edu/admissions/mba

WHERE TO FIND $100,000+ JOBS ON THE WEB

http://www.theladders.com

This job search service for the $100k+ segment of the employment marketplace was founded by Marc Cenedella, the former Senior Vice President of Finance and Operations at HotJobs.com. Investors in the site include several CEOs and a group of private investors from the banking and technology industries. Corporate executives laud the site for providing a valuable resource for those higher-level employees looking for new opportunities.

Prospective job seekers are notified of openings via the service's weekly newsletters, which are industry-specific to sales, marketing, and finance. Companies can search the Internet for job postings, or the employers can list them free of charge. Besides the free newsletter, TheLadders.com also offers a more in-depth, paid, premium service, all of which serves to filter out unqualified candidates and maintain the site's high standards of credibility—a great motivation for employers when searching for applicants.

HundredK.com
http://www.hundredk.com
info@hundredk.com

This site, founded in 2001 but only online since 2003, publishes thousands of executive jobs annually. It is one of the largest online centers for $100K+ job searching and recruiting. The jobs they list typically come directly from executive recruiters and corporate contacts; therefore, many of their job listings (the site claims as many as 95%) cannot be found on a free job site. All listings are investigated before being posted to verify authenticity and salary (no jobs with an annual salary of $100,000 will be listed). An interesting additional feature allows executives and professionals who are not actively job seeking to post their anonymous profile and resume for free, which then becomes available to recruiters.

BEST METRO AREAS TO LAUNCH A BUSINESS OR CAREER

As this list proves, location is always important, but not necessarily in the way we might think. According to Forbes.com, smaller areas which are relatively distant from big cities typically offer lower operation and living costs. They are also often near universities, which offer a diverse, educated work force.

- Madison, WI
- Raleigh-Durham, NC
- Austin, TX
- Washington, DC
- Atlanta, GA

- Provo, UT
- Boise, ID
- Huntsville, AL
- Lexington, KY
- Richmond, VA

TOP TEN COMPANIES IN THE WORLD RANKED BY SALES

According to Forbes.com, to qualify for the *Forbes* A-List of the finest large corporations in the world, companies must demonstrate the ability to expand their sales and income in order to earn profits that will reward shareholders over the long haul. Companies must have annual sales of $5 billion or a stock market value of $5 billion. The *Forbes* staff then looks at a variety of data including five-year sales, profit and return on capital data, and recent stock market performance to whittle down the list.

- Wal-Mart Stores
- Total Fina Elf
- NTT
- Siemens
- Allianz

- Carrefour
- Home Depot
- Peugeot
- AIG
- Unilever

10 OF AMERICA'S LARGEST PRIVATELY HELD COMPANIES

F*orbes* annually releases a list of top ten privately owned companies, which are much like Trump's own company. Herein is a list as presented by *Forbes* for the year 2004. For the last five years, 14 companies have traded the top ten spots. Regardless, these companies are filled with teams of the best, hardworking, entrepreneurial executives in the country, who are handsomely remunerated for their innovations and accomplishments.

1. Cargill
   PO Box 9300, Minneapolis, MN 55440
   phone 952-742-7575 fax 952-742-7393
   URL: http://www.cargill.com
   CEO: Warren R Staley CFO: Robert L Lumpkins
Cargill is America's largest privately-held firm. The company, which sells agricultural and industrial products, employs over 98,000 people in 61 countries.

2. Koch Industries
   4111 East 37th Street North, Wichita, KS 67220
   phone 316-828-5500   fax 316-828-5739
   URL: http://www.kochind.com
   E-mail: info@kochind.com
   CEO: Charles Koch   CFO: Steve Feilmeier
Koch Industries owns a diverse group of companies
engaged in trading, petroleum, asphalt, natural gas, gas
liquids, chemicals, plastics and fibers, chemical technology
equipment, minerals, fertilizers, ranching, securities and
finance.

3. Mars
   6885 Elm Street, McLean, VA 22101
   phone 703-821-4900   fax 703-448-9678
   URL: http://www.mars.com
   E-mail: contact.us@mars.com
   CEO: Benno Hoogendoorn
Known for their brand name candies such as 3 Musketeers,
M&Ms, Milky Way, Snickers, and Skittles, Mars is also
behind such products as Pedigree and Whiskas. The
company has offices and facilities in over 60 countries and
has been in operation since 1911.

4. Publix Super Markets
   3300 Airport Road, Lakeland, FL 33811
   phone 863-413-8185   fax 863-284-5532
   URL: http://www.publix.com
   CEO: Charles H Jenkins Jr   CFO: David Phillips
Publix is the largest employee-owned supermarket chain in

the U.S. and operates 787 retail food supermarkets throughout Florida, Georgia, South Carolina, Alabama and Tennessee.

5. PricewaterhouseCoopers
   1177 Avenue of the Americas, New York, NY 10036
   phone 646-471-4000 fax 646-471-3188
   URL: http://www.pwcglobal.com
   CEO: Samuel A DiPiazza Jr CFO: Marsha R Cohen
   PricewaterhouseCoopers was formed through the merger of Price Waterhouse and Coopers & Lybrand in 1998 and refers to the U.S. firm of PricewaterhouseCoopers LLP and other members of the worldwide PricewaterhouseCoopers organization. It provides assurance, auditing, financial advice, human resource solutions, and tax services to clients in 140 countries.

6. Ernst & Young
   5 Times Square, New York, NY 10036
   phone 212-773-3000 fax 212-773-6350
   URL: http://www.ey.com
   E-mail: webmaster@ey.com
   CEO: James S Turley CFO: Jeffrey Dworken
   Ernst & Young, with over 106,000 people in more than 140 countries, is a global provider of professional services and financial reporting. Their services include audit, tax, and corporate finance.

7. Bechtel
   P.O. Box 193965, San Francisco, CA 94119-3965
   phone 415-768-1234 fax 415-768-9038

URL: http://www.bechtel.com
E-mail: webmstr@bechtel.com
CEO: Riley P Bechtel   CFO: Peter Dawson
Bechtel was founded in 1898 and is engaged in a wide variety of projects in civil infrastructure, power, telecommunications and government services. The company's notable projects include the Channel Tunnel connecting England and France and Hong Kong International Airport. Currently the company is working on the Boston Central Artery/Tunnel (Big Dig), the Waste Treatment Immobilization Plant at the Department of Energy's Hanford site in Washington, and rebuilding infrastructure in Iraq.

8. C&S Wholesale Grocers
   47 Old Ferry Road, Brattleboro, VT 05302
   phone 802-257-4371   fax 802-257-6857
   URL: http://www.cswg.com
   CEO: Richard B Cohen   CFO: Mark Gross
The company was founded in 1918 and is a broad line distributor of food to supermarkets, retail stores and military bases. They serve approximately 5,000 stores via warehouses in Vermont, Maine, Massachusetts, Connecticut, Rhode Island, New York, New Jersey, Pennsylvania, Maryland, Ohio, California and Hawaii.

9. Meijer
   2929 Walker Avenue, NW, Grand Rapids, MI 49544
   phone 616-453-6711   fax 616-791-5346
   URL: http://www.meijer.com
   E-mail: webmaster@meijer.com

CEO: Hank Meijer   CFO: Jim Walsh
Meijer was founded in 1934 and is a large grocery and merchandise chain in the Midwest, with 158 combination superstores in five states (Illinois, Indiana, Kentucky, Michigan, and Ohio). The stores include such specialty departments as auto supplies, electronics, nutrition centers and floral departments.

10. HE Butt Grocery
    646 South Main Avenue, San Antonio, TX 78204
    phone 210-938-8000   fax 210-938-8213
    URL: http://www.heb.com
    E-mail: customer.relations@heb.com
    CEO: Charles C Butt   CFO: Jack Brouillard
HE Butt Grocery Company is a regional supermarket chain operating 304 stores in Texas and northern Mexico. It runs one of the largest milk and bread processing plants in the Southwest and also has facilities producing ice cream, yogurt and other food products. In addition, the company has its own photofinishing operations. HEB gives 5% of its pretax earnings to public and charitable causes.

BUSINESS WEB RESOURCES

The following list of Business Web Resources was obtained from the American Library Association's Business Reference and Services Section: "Best of the Best Business Web Sites." American Library Association. 2003. *(26 May, 2004 http://www.ala.org/rusa/brass/besthome.html)*

ACCOUNTING

Rutgers Accounting Web (RAW)
http://raw.rutgers.edu/
RAW is the most well-known accounting site on the Web. It has many useful features for students and researchers, including service providers and career opportunities. Some tax information is also available.

AICPA Online
http://www.aicpa.org/
The American Institute of Certified Public Accountants

(AICPA) is a professional association for accountants. Their Web site gives association news, developments, and career opportunities, as well as links to selected sites.

SmartPros
http://accounting.smartpros.com
Professional accountants looking for news, products, and new opportunities stop here first. This site contains vast lists of international, federal and state information, as well as associations, educational information, and a glossary.

TAXATION
Tax and Accounting Sites Directory
http://www.taxsites.com/

This site is a comprehensive index of tax, accounting, and related resources on the Internet. It is especially useful for novices who are searching the Web for tax and accounting information.

Statistics of Income
http://www.irs.ustreas.gov/
This program produces data files compiled from tax and information returns filed with the IRS. Among other features, the site provides downloadable files of statistics from researchers looking for projections and aggregated data regarding corporations, individuals, employment taxes, and partnerships.

ADVERTISING AND MARKETING

Advertising Age
http://www.adage.com/
This is a well-established industry publication whose website provides a number of useful links for researchers.

Advertising World
http://advertising.utexas.edu/world/
This site was created by the University of Texas at Austin's Advertising Department and is an exhaustive collection of links to advertising and marketing information, in over 81 categories and including many hard-to-locate topics.

CI Strategies and Tools: I3 Internet Intelligence Index (Fuld & Company)
http://www.fuld.com/i3/index.html
This is an excellent site for obtaining marketing data for specific industries.

CyberAtlas
http://cyberatlas.internet.com/
This site provides a collection of facts online which have been obtained from secondary sources. The site includes and archive of statistical data and a glossary of commonly used technical terms.

GVU's WWW User Surveys
http://www.gvu.gatech.edu/user_surveys/
This website provides results of surveys that have been periodically produced by the Georgia Tech's College of Computing. Survey results provide data, graphs, and charts and are arranged into detailed categories.

Know Marketing: The Internet's Marketing Virtual Library
http://www.knowthis.com/
This virtual library supplies web resources on a wealth of topics, including advertising, selling, promotion, research, and electronic commerce.

FINANCIAL DATA
Electronic Data Gathering Analysis and Retrieval (EDGAR) 1994-
http://www.sec.gov/edgarhp.htm
Provides 10-K, 20-F, proxy statements, annual reports, and other financial statements of public companies filed with the Securities and Exchange Commission.

Yahoo! Finance
http://finance.yahoo.com
This Yahoo! site links to information on U.S. markets, world markets, data sources, finance references, investment editorials, financial news, and other helpful Web sites.

Stockmaster
http://www.stockmaster.com/
This site provides extensive investment information, including quotes, news, SEC filings, and earnings histories. A helpful search feature allows queries by company name or ticker symbol.

Holt Stock Report
http://metro.turnpike.net/holt/index.html
Through daily reports, this site provides market summaries

for 29 indexes and averages for domestic and international markets. Their archive goes back to 1994.

Public Register's Annual Report Service
http://www.prars.com/
This, the largest annual report service in America, provides free company financials on over 3,600 public companies.

DIRECTORIES
Companies Online
http://www.CompaniesOnline.com/
This database allows you to locate more than 75,000 companies using name, location, or type of business.

Hoover's Corporate Register
http://www.hoovers.com
This site gives links to company home pages. It also has a subscription service portion that contains profiles for 10,000 major companies. The profiles include contact information, a review of the company, and more.

Fortune 500
http://www.pathfinder.com/fortune/companies/
This list of links can be searched by company or in various ranking orders.

Forbes 500
http://forbes.com/tool/html/toolbox.htm
Search this popular site by any of its famous rankings, including the "Forbes 500," the "Best 200 Small Businesses,"

the "Top 40 Financial Companies," and the "International 500."

PR Newswire (*http://www.prnewswire.com*) and Business Wire (*http://www.businesswire.com*)
Electronic wire services like these allow you to access corporate press releases and other news stories that often never make it into print.

BUSINESS ETHICS

Better Business Bureau Online
http://www.bbb.org/
The best site for checking the reputation of businesses, it also includes a charity report.

Business Ethics Resources on WWW
http://www.ethicsweb.ca/
A comprehensive list of web resources compiled by the Centre for Applied Ethics.

CorpWatch
http://www.corpwatch.org/
This site provides news, opinion papers, and alerts on global corporate activities.

ELECTRONIC COMMERCE

E-commerce
(Nanyang Technological University Library)
http://www.ntu.edu.sg/library/mktg/ecomm.htm

This guide provides a wealth of links for electronic commerce.

EMarketer
http://www.emarketer.com/
Created as a one-stop resource for electronic commerce, this site provides information and resources for building, promoting, and maintaining a successful electronic commerce website.

FINANCIAL MARKETS AND INVESTMENTS
Virtual Finance Library
http://www.cob.ohio-state.edu/dept/fin/overview.htm
Created by Ohio State's Department of Finance, this Web site covers most investment areas, including information about equities, bonds, money markets, insurance, currencies, investment banks, and macroeconomics information.

FinWeb.com
http://finweb.com
Created by James R. Graven at Louisiana State University, FinWeb's primary objective is to list Internet resources providing substantive information concerning economics and finance related topics.

CNNFN
http://cnnfn.com
Produced by CNNFN, this web site provides stories concerning business news, personal finance, and global financial markets.

Investor Information
http://www.sec.gov/investor.shtml
Created by the Securities and Exchange Commission Office
of Investor Education and Assistance, this page has links to
SEC tips and publications that will help you to "invest wise-
ly and avoid costly mistakes and fraud."

Bonds Online
http://www.bondsonline.com/
Site includes information on U.S. corporate bonds, bond
funds, convertible bonds, and much more.

Monthly Statement of the Public Debt of the United States
http://www.publicdebt.treas.gov/bpd/bpdindex.htm
This site provides the monthly data for treasury bills, notes,
and other federal securities.

MUTUAL FUNDS
ICI Mutual Fund Connection
http://www.ici.org
Published by the Investment Company Institute, this
informative site enhances public understanding of the
investment company industry and the policy issues that
affect it, particularly those involving legislation and regula-
tion, the U.S. economy, and retirement security.

Mutual Fund Fact Book
http://www.ici.org/stats/mf/2003_factbook.pdf
Contains an overview of what a mutual fund is, the trends,

and the various mutual fund investment objectives. The statistics section includes fund assets, sales, and portfolio purchases.

Mutual Fund Investor's Center
http://www.mfea.com/
Published by the Mutual Fund Education Alliance, the not-for-profit trade association of the no-load mutual fund industry, this resource is designed to serve as an important resource for investors who want to use mutual funds to reach their financial goals.

COMMODITIES AND FUTURES
Commodity Futures Trading Commission
http://www.cftc.gov/cftc/cftchome.htm
Commodity Futures Trading Commission (CFTC) is an independent agency with the mandate to regulate commodity futures and option markets in the United States. The Web site has links to all domestic exchanges, market analysis, market surveillance, and market research.

FAOSTAT Agriculture Data
1961-
http://www.fao.org/waicent/search/default.asp
Made available by the Food & Agriculture Organization of the United Nations, FAOSTAT provides statistical compilation on agricultural production and trade on both a world wide and country by country basis for all types of crops, livestock, and agricultural commodities.

GENERAL MANAGEMENT

Business Researcher's Interests
http://brint.com/interest.html
One of the most comprehensive business web sites, this site links to numerous sites that deal with various aspects of management.

Management Link
http://www.inst-mgt.org.uk/external/mgt-menu.html
Extensive list of links to management sites.

Institute of Management and Administration's (IOMA) Business Management Supersite
http://www.ioma.com/
Sample articles from their 40 business management newsletters and salary survey information.

American Management Association International homepage
http://www.amanet.org/
This non-profit educational organization publishes a variety of print and electronic media to promote organizational effectiveness.

HUMAN RESOURCE MANAGEMENT AND LABOR RELATIONS
Employment and Benefits Law
http://www.willyancey.com/emp_law.htm
Contains links to many resources on such topics as employment law, labor-management relations, labor standards, and employee rights and responsibilities.

National Labor Relations Board
http://www.nlrb.gov/
NLRB primarily guards employees against unfair labor practices by employers or unions and oversees elections where employees decide whether they want to be represented by unions.

SRHM Online
http://www.shrm.org/
The Society for Human Resource Management provides a vast amount of information related to Human Resources.

United States Equal Employment Opportunity Commission
http://www.eeoc.gov/
The EEOC enforces employment discrimination laws and conducts investigations of alleged discrimination in the workplace. The page provides useful information for both employees and employers alike.

INTERNATIONAL BUSINESS

CIA World Factbook
http://www.odci.gov/cia/publications/factbook/
Published by the U.S. Central Intelligence Agency, this online counterpart contains economic, social, and political country profiles of countries.

Europages: The European Business Directory
http://www.europages.com/home-en.html
A multilingual directory site of 500,000 companies in 30 European countries searchable by product, company name

or business sector. There are links to European business sites.

GLOBUS & NTDB
http://www.stat-usa.gov/tradtest.nsf
Subscription-based one-stop site for information and trade leads from the U.S. National Trade Data Bank (NTDB). Sections include trade news, current exchange rates, market and country research, international trade statistics, and current press releases. Of particular note are International Marketing Insight (IMI) Reports.

International Chamber of Commerce
http://www.iccwbo.org
The International Chamber of Commerce (ICC) is the world business organization. It links global chamber organizations and committees by country.

International Trade Administration
http://www.ita.doc.gov/
Developed and maintained by International Trade Administration (ITA), U.S. Department of Commerce, this site includes a wealth of information on trade and industry statistics, market data, exporting, importing, and Big Emerging Markets (BEMs).

OECD Online
http://www.oecd.org
Home page of the Organization for Economic Co-operation and Development (OECD). Member governments collect data, monitor trends, analyze and forecast economic developments and also research social changes and trade patterns.

World Bank
http://www.worldbank.org
The World Bank Group site contains development reports, resources on global economics and trade, and country and regional information. Current research projects and information on international development loans and activities are also included.

SMALL BUSINESS

Entrepreneur.Com: The Online Small Business Authority
http://www.entrepreneurmag.com
Maintained by Entrepreneur Magazine to support new business ideas and growing companies, it contains selected articles from the publication and resources for business developers.

Entrepreneurial Edge Online
http://www.lowe.org
Homepage of the Edward Lowe Foundation, devoted to championing the entrepreneurial spirit.

Entrepreneur's Reference Guide to Small Business Information
http://www.loc.gov/rr/business/guide/guide2.html
The 2nd edition of a guide compiled by the staff of the Business Reference Services' Science, Technology, and Business Division, Library of Congress.

Entreworld
Kauffman Center for Entrepreneurial Leadership

http://www.entreworld.com
This site includes a wide range of subjects divided into three categories: Starting Your Business, Growing Your Business, and Supporting Entrepeneurship.

Fambiz.Com
http://fambiz.com
This site tailors its information to family-controlled companies.

Idea Cafe: The Small Business Channel
http://www.businessownersideacafe.com
Developed by successful entrepreneurs and authors of published guides on forming and running a business, this site includes resources, ideas, practical advice, business news, and humor. Business site links are summarized and reviewed.

Patent Cafe
http://www.patentcafe.com
Information from the "World's Gateway to Inventor's Resources" includes patents and trademarks, resources for invention and innovation, and manufacturers and suppliers.

SCORE (Service Corps of Retired Executives)
http://www.score.org
The SCORE organization is a resource partner with the U.S. Small Business Administration. It is dedicated to aiding in the formation, growth and success of small business nationwide. The organization offers counseling and workshops to business owners.

U.S. Small Business Administration
http://www.sba.gov
Starting point for resources and programs offered by the SBA.

Women's Business Center
http://www.onlinewbc.gov/
This interactive business training web site was created in partnership with the U.S. Small Business Administration's Office of Women's Business Ownership, and is useful for entrepreneurial women dedicated to the development of professional and personal skills.

RECOMMENDED READING

BOOKS BY DONALD TRUMP

Trump: The Way to the Top: The Best Business Advice I Ever Received, Crown, May 2004.
This collection of wisdom and advice from the business elite includes valuable advice for businesspeople at any level.

Trump: How to Get Rich (with Meredith McIver), Random House, March 2004.
In this candid book, Donald Trump reveals the secrets of his success.

The America We Deserve (with Dave Shiflett), Renaissance Books, January 2000.
In plainspoken fashion, Donald Trump discusses his vision of America's future.

Trump: The Art of the Comeback, Crown Business, October 1997.
In the major recession of 1990, many real estate moguls experienced financial catastrophe. In this revealing book, Trump tells how he

survived that difficult time and emerged as a great success.

Trump: Surviving at the Top, Random House, August 1990.
Donald Trump explains how he has maintained his success.

Trump: The Art of the Deal (with Tony Schwartz), Random House,
November 1987.
This classic personal history reveals the inside world of Donald Trump.

BOOKS ABOUT DONALD TRUMP AND HIS FAMILY

Baida, Peter. *Poor Richard's Legacy: American Business Values from
Benjamin Franklin to Donald Trump*. New York: William Morrow,
1990.
This social history profiles business giants, illustrating the modern
downfall of American business ethics.

Barrett, Wayne. *Trump: The Deals and the Downfall*. New York:
HarperCollins, 1992.
In this fascinating biography, investigative reporter Barrett
thoroughly chronicles Trump's life.

Blair, Gwenda. *The Trumps: Three Generations That Built an Empire*.
New York: Simon & Schuster, 2000.
Journalist Gwenda Blair explores the life of three generations of
Trumps—Donald Trump's grandfather, Friedrich, a German-born
barber who founded the family real estate empire in Queens; Donald
Trump's father, Fred, who utilized new government programs to
create affordable housing that brought him great profits; and
Donald, himself.

Brallier, Jess M. and Richard P. McDonough. *The Really, Really Classy
Donald Trump Quiz Book: Complete, Unauthorized, Fantastic...and
the Best*. New York: Little Brown & Company, 1990.
This hilarious book is filled with fun quizzes about the business
giant.

Hurt, Harry and Harvey Hurt. *Lost Tycoon: The Many Lives of Donald J. Trump*. New York: W. W. Norton & Company, 1993.
Based on court records and sources within the Trump organization, this book reveals all aspects of Trump's empire.

O'Donnell, John R., James Rutherford, and Pat Towle. *Trumped! The Inside Story of the Real Donald Trump—His Cunning Rise and Spectacular Fall*. New York: Simon & Schuster, 1991.
This evenhanded biography tells the intriguing story of the life of Donald Trump.

Reed, Joel M. *Trump: The Man, the Myth, the Scandal*. Masquerade Books, 1990.

Tuccille, Jerome. *Trump: The Saga of America's Most Powerful Real Estate Baron*. Beard Group, 2004.

RECOMMENDED READING—LEADERSHIP AND MANAGEMENT

Blanchard, Kenneth H. and Spencer Johnson. *The One Minute Manager*. New York: William Morrow, 1982.
Millions of American managers have successfully followed this book's techniques for more than twenty years.

Bossidy, Larry, with Charles Burck and Ram Charan. *Execution: The Discipline of Getting Things Done*. New York: Crown Publishing, 2002.
Developing strategy is always more exciting than actually getting things done, and in this insightful book the authors explain how the ability to execute plans is what really creates success.

Brooks, William T. *The New Science of Selling and Persuasion: How Smart Companies and Great Salespeople Sell*. Hoboken, New Jersey: John Wiley & Sons, 2004.
This book reveals the secrets to selling in the twenty-first century,

and illustrates how to update simplistic, outdated sales practices.

Buckingham, Marcus and Curt Coffman. *First, Break All the Rules.*
New York: Simon & Schuster, 1999.
Based on a quarter-decade's worth of interviews, the authors debunk
many standard management concepts, such as "treat people as you
like to be treated" and "people are capable of almost anything."

Buckingham, Marcus and Donald O. Clifton. *Now, Discover Your
Strengths.* New York: Free Press, 2001.
This book offers a revolutionary approach to managing personnel—
rather than attempting to eliminate their weaknesses, focus on
enhancing their strengths.

Collins, Jim. *Good to Great: Why Some Companies Make the
Leap...and Others Don't.* New York: HarperCollins, 2001.
In this essential book for any CEO, Jim Collins explains the
common traits that have propelled businesses to great success.

Johnson, Spencer. *Who Moved My Cheese? An Amazing Way to Deal
with Change in Your Work and in Your Life.* New York: Putnam, 1998.
This parable, illustrating the nature of change and how it can play an
important role in corporate life, has become a business classic.

Lencioni, Patrick M. *The Five Dysfunctions of a Team: A Leadership
Fable.* Jossey-Bass, 2002.
This entertaining fable, filled with useful information, targets group
behavior and shows how the basic elements of teamwork are necessary
for success.

Lundin, Stephen C., John Christensen and Harry Paul. *Fish! A
Remarkable Way to Boost Morale and Improve Results.* New York:
Hyperion, 2000.
This management parable is about Seattle fishmongers who help a
troubled businesswoman turn her company around.

Maxwell, John C., edited by Rolf Zettersten. *The 21 Indispensable Qualities of a Leader: Becoming the Person That People Want to Follow.* Thomas Nelson, 1999.
Why do some people seem natural leaders, and others do not? This book identifies the 21 "character qualities" successful leaders possess.

RECOMMENDED READING—BUSINESS BIOGRAPHIES

Arax, Mark. *The King of California: J. G. Boswell and the Making of a Secret American Empire.* New York: Perseus Publishing, 2003.
J. G. Boswell controls the biggest American farming empire, worth more than $1 billion. After moving from Georgia to California in the early 1900s, the Boswells planted the cotton that would make their fortune. This book follows the family from the 1800s to the present day.

Byron, Christopher M. Testosterone Inc: *Tales of CEOs Gone Wild.* Hoboken, New Jersey: John Wiley & Sons, 2004.
Since the 1990s, CEOs have often become celebrities in their own right. Christopher Byron delves into the personal lives of some of these business icons, revealing what they really do in their free time.

Eisner, Michael D. *Work in Progress: Risking Failure, Surviving Success.* New York: Hyperion, 1999.
This memoir tells the true story of the Disney CEO.

Harman, Sidney. *Mind Your Own Business.* New York: Doubleday & Company, 2003.
Sidney Harman, CEO of Harman International, shares his revolutionary ideas about leadership in this compelling autobiography.

Langley, Monica. *Tearing Down the Walls: How Sandy Weill Fought His Way to the Top of the Financial World...and Then Nearly Lost It All.* New York: Simon & Schuster, 2003.

This biography of Sandy Weill, the CEO of Citigroup, shows how Weill became such a prominent figure in the finance and business worlds.

Lewis, Michael. *Liar's Poker: Rising Through the Wreckage on Wall Street*. New York: Penguin, 1990.
This memoir describes Michael Lewis's four years with the Wall Street firm Salomon Brothers, revealing the game-mentality that plagues the Street today.

McDougal, Dennis. *Privileged Son: Otis Chandler and the Rise and Fall of the L. A. Times Dynasty*. New York: Perseus, 2001.
This biography of the enigmatic Otis Chandler, the last Chandler to head the L.A. Times, also includes a thorough history of the renowned paper.

Shames, Laurence and Peter Barton. *Not Fade Away: A Short Life Well Lived*. Rodale Press, 2003.
This illuminating memoir reveals the life of Peter Barton, the pivotal figure in the creation of cable television.

Welch, Jack and John A. Byrne. *Jack: Straight from the Gut*. New York: Warner Books, 2001.
This memoir by the General Electric CEO describes his meteoric rise up the corporate ladder.

Woodward, Bob. *Maestro: Greenspan's Fed and the American Boom*. New York: Simon & Schuster, 2000.
This absorbing biography of the Federal Reserve chairman is perfect for those interested in politics and business.

RECOMMENDED READING—SALES & MARKETING

Alsop, Ronald J. *The 18 Immutable Laws of Corporate Reputation: Creating, Protecting, and Repairing Your Most Valuable Asset*. Wall Street Journal Books, 2004.

Ronald Alsop, a reputation management expert, explains how to protect corporate reputations in an increasingly suspicious business climate.

Blanchard, Ken. *Raving Fans: A Revolutionary Approach to Customer Service.* New York: William Morrow & Co., 1993.
This parable explains how, in order to truly succeed, a business has to create more than satisfied customers—they have to create raving fans.

Brooks, William T. *The New Science of Selling and Persuasion: How Smart Companies and Great Salespeople Sell.* Hoboken, New Jersey: John Wiley & Sons, 2004.
This book reveals the secrets to selling in the twenty-first century, and illustrates how to update simplistic, outdated sales practices.

Fox, Jeffrey J. *How to Become a Marketing Superstar: Unexpected Rules That Ring the Cash Register.* Hyperion, 2003.
This snappy advice book shows readers how to solve real-life business problems.

Fox, Jeffrey J. *How to Become a Rainmaker: The Rules for Getting and Keeping Customers and Clients.* Hyperion, 2000.
This commonsense guide explains how to maintain a successful sales process.

Gitomer, Jeffrey. *The Patterson Principles of Selling.* Hoboken, New Jersey: John Wiley & Sons, 2004.
These practical selling principles have been consistently successful since John Patterson developed them in the 1880s.

Mandino, Og. *The Greatest Salesman in the World.* New York: Bantam Doubleday Dell, 1974.
First published in 1968, this clear, helpful parable combines mythology and spirituality into a classic text on the philosophy of salesmanship.

Moore, Geoffrey A. *Crossing the Chasm: Marketing and Selling High-Tech Products to Mainstream Customers.* New York: HarperCollins, 2002.
This invaluable guide shows how to market high-tech products.

Ries, Al. *Positioning: The Battle for Your Mind.* McGraw-Hill, 2000.
This book shows how to properly position your company in the mind of potential customers.

Smith, Benson. *Discover Your Sales Strengths: How the World's Greatest Salespeople Develop Winning Careers.* New York: Warner Books, 2003.
An explanation of how there is no single recipe for success, this guide helps readers find their own, individual way to be a good salesperson.

ABOUT THE AUTHORS

Anthony Parinello is the *Wall Street Journal* bestselling author of five books, including *Selling to VITO™: The Very Important Top Officer* and *Secrets of VITO™: Think and Sell Like a CEO.*

Beth Gottfried is a Boston-based writer who writes a regular column on *The Apprentice* for www.the-trades.com.